DEAD GIVEAWAY

CHARLES RAMSEY
DEAD GIVEAWAY

The Rescue, Hamburgers, White Folks, and Instant Celebrity ... What You Saw on TV Doesn't Even *Begin* to Tell the Story ...

WITH RANDY NYERGES

GRAY & COMPANY, PUBLISHERS
CLEVELAND

To Ashely, the love of my life

© 2014 by Charles Ramsey with Randy Nyerges

Gray & Company, Publishers
www.grayco.com

ISBN: 978-1-938441-51-6

Printed in U.S.A.
1

CONTENTS

DEAD GIVEAWAY

INTRODUCTION

MAY 6, 2013, IS a day that will forever be etched in Cleveland's history—and my own. It started out just like any other day, but by evening time the world's attention zeroed in on the house just a few feet away from mine. Without warning or as much as a moment to prepare, world attention then came down on me like a shower of anvils. In a matter of minutes, my world turned upside down that sunny afternoon.

When the news broke that three young women who had been missing for a decade had just been found, alive, the city of Cleveland, a city that longs for moments to celebrate, suddenly became Party Central. Hundreds, perhaps thousands, of people took to the streets in the kind of mass celebration you would expect to see if the Indians, Browns, or Cavaliers won a world title. Within minutes, national and international news media picked up the story, and then folks all over the world joined in the celebration, too.

Because of my small part in the story, a lot of people seemed to become fascinated with me.

People who write books about their life experiences usually try to show their better side. They tell their story the way they want it to be remembered. The real truth behind the story often gets pushed off to the side, or buried among self-serving or insignificant details. And by the end of the story, you wind up liking the person telling it. Can you think of any self-written story or book where you end up disliking the person? I can't. But this book may change that.

In this book, it is my goal to be honest, brutally honest, about myself and others who played a part in how I became what I am. I reveal many warts, some of them oozy and very hairy. I give my honest opinion about what happened that day and the crazy weeks and months that followed. I give some very politically incorrect views without the cream and sugar. I talk about my upbringing, and pull no punches as to how this privileged suburban kid jumped the tracks and damn near fucked everything up several times over. Sometimes others had a part in that, more often it was just me being me. Yet, through it all, I always found a way to laugh.

Just as a plane crash is usually the result of a bizarre series of unlikely events, it was a bizarre series of unlikely events that led to my involvement in the rescue of Amanda Berry, Gina DeJesus and Michelle Knight. In fact, my whole life has been a series of plane crashes. And usually the result of pilot error.

This story will make you laugh. It will make you cry. It will make you angry. It will surprise you. It may even insult you. But I didn't write it to make you feel good. I wrote it to poke you in the eye. To discuss the real world. To make you question the way things are and the way you think.

For some reason, God put me in the wrong place at the right time that fateful spring day. I'm glad so many people's lives have been changed for the better, and, perhaps in some way this experience will change mine.

Charles Ramsey Jr.

April 2014

THE RESCUE

SOMEBODY HAD TO PEEL a hundred pounds of onions every day, and that job almost always fell on me.

I had been working at Hodge's restaurant in Cleveland for seven months. I enjoyed working the 4-to-close shift because it was more laid back (and if I were asked to prep 20 steaks, no one minded if I prepped 21). I was a lowly dishwasher, but I showed up for work every day, did what I was told, and paid attention to the details. My bills were paid.

But French onion soup and French onion ravioli were very popular items on the menu, and that meant a lot of onions. I loathed onion-peeling duty. It's hard enough on your eyes to peel and chop *one* onion. But I had to peel, slice, and chop *one hundred pounds*. I'd rather skin a hippopotamus.

This particular day was one hundred pounds too many.

"That's it," I yelled to Jim, the executive chef. "I'm sick and tired of putting up with this shit. The next sonofabitch who doesn't help me peel these onions is gonna get peeled by me." I slammed the knife down on the table and stormed off.

For probably the millionth time in my life, my big mouth (which now had a big gap because I'd recently lost my front tooth when biting into an apple) got me into trouble. Jim—the boss—called me into his office.

"Chuck, you're really starting to frighten me," he said. "We just can't have that kind of behavior in the kitchen."

"Oh, come on," I said. "I was just letting off a little steam. I'm not about to do anything to anyone. No big deal, man."

"That's not the ethics we want around here," Jim said.

"Ethics?" I asked. "You don't seem to have a problem with ethics when we call each other 'nigger' around here."

I went back to peeling those damn onions.

But about a week later we had another run-in. I was leaning over to wipe down a table when a brass cartridge slipped out of my pocket out onto the table. It was a spent shell casing from an AK-47 assault rifle. A friend of mine who served in Iraq had given it to me.

Jim called me into his office again.

"Go home, Chuck. You're off for two weeks." He told me I was perceived as a "threat."

Hell, any knife I might pick up while clearing a table could do a lot more damage than a spent cartridge. What did he think I was going to do with that bitch, throw it at someone's eye?

*   *   *

On Monday, May 6, 2013, I got up early like I usually do. This was the last day of my suspension, and I was worried about how I was going to make the $75-a-week rent without those two $269-a-week paychecks. One thing I was sure of, at least: A few stints in the penitentiary had long cured me of any desire to sell drugs again.

I watched some TV, putzed around the house, surfed the Internet on my Samsung smart phone (which now sits on the bottom of the Hudson River—more about that later). Eventually I heard the familiar soft clanging of the mailbox as the mailman made his delivery to the boarding house I shared with two other guys at 2203 Seymour Avenue. I stepped onto the porch, flipped open the lid, and looked through the mail. One piece of mail didn't belong to me, but I saw the guy who it belonged to standing in his driveway.

"Hey, Ariel! That mailman brought me some of your mail again," I said. For some reason, the mailman frequently put pieces of his mail in my box and pieces of my mail in his box.

"Geeze, I need to just move in with you guys," Ariel Castro said in his charming Puerto Rican accent, a smile outlined by his salt-and-pepper beard. He was wearing his usual white shirt, black jeans, leather motorcycle jacket covering a tattoo on his left bicep, brown construction boots, dark shades, with a fisherman's cap topping off his pudgy 5-foot-8 frame. I stepped off my rickety porch and handed it to him.

Ariel Castro seemed like a normal, regular good neighbor. He pretty much kept to himself, but when we saw each other we always said hi. He would often barbeque in his back yard and we'd share some ribs, pork chops, burgers, and chicken. The dude could cook with the finest Puerto Rican flair. Just the right combination of spices and fiery habanero pepper. With spring beginning to take hold in Cleveland, I was looking forward to more evenings of that sweet smoky odor wafting from his yard into mine.

"The hotter the music, the hotter the food," Ariel would always say. Sometimes he had his granddaughter, or who I thought was his granddaughter, over for his cookouts, saying that he wanted to "Americanize her."

Ariel referred to everything good as "*muy caliente*." The food was *muy caliente*. A nice day was *muy caliente*. The salsa music he liked to play was *muy caliente*.

*   *   *

A bit after five that afternoon I fumbled through the remaining $11 in my pocket and giddily concluded I had more than enough for a Big Mac meal. It was a bright, brilliant, sunny, late afternoon, so I thought I'd hop on my Schwinn mountain bike (which I bought off some crackhead for $10) and pedal to my local McDonald's at West 32nd Street and Clark Avenue.

"Hey Poppy, what can I get you today?" the polite Puerto Rican kid asked as I squared up to the counter. "Big Mac, medium fries, small Sprite," I said. My usual order. The kid quickly gave me my change, gathered my order, and pushed the white bag across the counter. "Thanks, bro," I said as I made my way out the door and back to my Schwinn, which fortunately was still where I left it.

I made my way east on Clark, and just before I hung a right on West 25th Street a couple of dudes in the parking lot of the Family Dollar store called out to me.

"Yo, Poppy, you wanna buy a pit bull puppy? Twenty dollar." They had a cardboard box in the back of the car, and out of curiosity I cruised over there.

"Whadaya got there?" I asked.

"Pit bull puppies," one of the dudes said, pulling open the top of the box.

I looked in. Obviously these idiots were trying to capitalize on the status and home security of owning a pit bull on west side of Cleveland, and they thought this black dude was a sucker sale.

"What pit bulls?" I laughed. "Those aren't no pit bulls. Those are Shih Tzus."

"Wha? No, them's pit bulls," the one dude tried to convince me.

Hey, I may be a dumb dishwasher, but I know the difference between a pit bull and a Shih Tzu. A Shih Tzu wouldn't last five minutes in a cockfight. I'm sure these morons probably stole those dogs from a pet store and thought they could pass them off as pit. bulls to someone dumber than them. So I just headed down West 25th and hung a left on Seymour. I rolled up on my house and parked my bike on my porch. I went in the house, took a seat on my porch, and took a bite into that juicy Big Mac. Life was tough, but it was good.

And then something happened that would change the lives of so many people in so many ways . . .

Sitting there, burger in hand, I heard a sudden banging from next door. At first I didn't know what to make of it, and I wanted my sandwich. But the banging continued. It got louder. Then I heard a woman's scream—the blood-curdling scream that you would hear if a kid got run over by a car.

"SOMEBODY HELP!"

Children playing on the street froze. Then more cries for help. I thought I'd seen Ariel go off to work, so I had not a clue as to what was going on. I looked outside and saw this Dominican dude, Angel Cordero, run across the street and onto the sidewalk. Without putting down my sandwich I ran to the sidewalk where Angel was standing.

BANG BANG BANG.

"Who the fuck is that?" I asked Angel.

"I don't know," Angel said, "but I'm not going up there."

I knew that Angel and Ariel didn't like each other, not for anything specific other than Angel was Dominican and Ariel was Puerto Rican. I guess that made them something like natural enemies within the Hispanic world, I don't know.

"Ok, I'm gonna check it out," I said. "You watch my back."

Big Mac still in hand, I ran up to Ariel's porch while Angel stayed behind. There was this young, attractive white woman, wearing a white tank top, clutching a child, lodged behind the storm door, banging and screaming.

"Get me out of here! Get me the fuck out of here!" she shrieked.

I was stunned. I had believed all this time that Ariel lived alone. I had never seen anyone over there other than him, other than the little girl I thought was his granddaughter. I figured this was some sort of domestic violence thing, a situation I was all too familiar with.

I stood on the porch. "How the hell did you get in there?" I asked this frantic woman. She had squeezed her left arm out from behind the storm door and was in no mood for a conversation.

"Just get me outta here!" she yelled.

I grabbed the storm door handle and yanked. Then I noticed the door was locked shut from the inside. I gave a couple more yanks, but that door wasn't going to budge. The girl gave the bottom panel a few meager kicks.

"Get the fuck back, bitch," I yelled. "I'm gonna kick the door in."

So I kicked that bottom panel with everything I had. Nothing. I picked my leg up and kicked it again, beating in the bottom panel of the aluminum door but not all the way. In my mind I knew I better act fast—not because it was time to be a hero, but because I was taking my own life into my hands. What do you think would have happened to me if a neighborhood of Puerto Ricans saw a scary-looking black dude trying to kick down the door of one of their fellow countrymen? I gave it one more size 13 kick and the panel broke inward. The girl crawled out and onto the porch, where I reached down to help her up. She got up, clutched onto me, then turned around and reached back through the busted bottom panel. The child was crying hysterically. The woman then pulled the diapered child through the bashed-in storm door. It was a little girl about six years old. She was screaming in terror.

But I recognized her! It was the little girl I had always believed was Ariel's granddaughter.

Ariel spent a fair amount of time working on his cars and motor-cycles in his backyard. He never cleaned up the oil or antifreeze that leaked all over the place. This little girl played with two oily dogs, a Chihuahua and a small white poodle, in Ariel's grimy back yard. I had always wondered why I only saw the little girl and never her mother or father.

"Can you shut this kid up?" I said, more annoyed than anything.

"She just wants her daddy," the girl said.

"Well then call the motherfucker!" I yelled.

"Ariel is her daddy," she said.

Now I was really confused. Ariel had a kid? And who was this pretty little white girl and how did she get here? Nothing made sense.

The girl turns to me and says, "Call 911. I'm Amanda Berry." At first, the name didn't ring a bell. It sounded like she said Linda something. My cell phone was sitting in my living room, so I told her to follow me. We stepped inside my house, and I spotted my phone. I picked it up and handed it to her.

Amanda looked at the phone in bewilderment. Little did I know she had been locked down in there for 10 years. Little did *she* know how to operate a touch-screen cell phone.

"I don't know how to work this," she said, still panicked, her daughter still screaming. I took the phone and punched in the three numbers, putting through a call that would literally be heard around the world. My language was coarse, but in a panic situation like this I didn't have time to refine my King's English.

The 911 operator answered, and I let it fly.

"I'm at 2207 Seymour, West 25th. Hey, check this out. I just came from McDonald's, right? I'm on my porch, eating my li'l food, right? This broad is tryin' to break out the fuckin' house next door to me. So, it's a bunch of people on the street right now and shit, so we like well, what's wrong? What's the problem? She like, 'This motherfucker done kidnapped me and my daughter and we been in this bitch.' She said her name was Linda Berry or some shit, I don't know who the fuck that is. I just moved over here, bro."

"Sir, sir, sir, sir. You have to calm down and slow down," the dispatcher said. "Is she still in the street?" Sorry to say this, but that operator was a fuckin' moron. I wasn't yelling or screaming or talking over him.

"Yeah, I'm lookin' at her. She callin' y'all. She on another phone."

I had told Amanda to call 911 herself because I was convinced that the police were going to think I was some screwball crazyass, especially after dealing with that moronic operator.

"Is she black, white, or Hispanic?"

"Uh, she white. But the baby look Hispanic."

"Okay, what is she wearing?"

"Uh, white tank top, light blue, uh, sweatpants. Like a wife-beater."

"Do you know the address next door? That she said she was in?"

"Yeah, 2207. I'm lookin' at it!"

"OK, I thought that was your address."

"Nah, I'm smarter than that, bro. I'm telling you where the crime was."

(At this point, the dispatcher asked for my name and phone number. When the Cleveland Police first released the 911 tape, this part was not edited out. Later, after the world had already heard it, most media outlets bleeped that out.)

"And the people she said that did this? Do you know if they still in the house?"

"I don't have a fuckin' clue, bro. I'm just standing here with my McDonald's."

The dispatcher asked if she needed an ambulance. I asked Amanda, and she said to send everything.

"She in a panic, bro. I think she been kidnapped so, you know, put yourself in her shoes."

"We'll send the police out."

"There you go!"

I'm gonna say this here once and only once. There have been several people on the news and on the Internet who said Angel Cordero ran up to the door and kicked it in. Others said this lady Aurora Marti, who lived across the street, ran up to the porch. They're all mistaken or fuckin' liars. Their motivation? Hard to say, but I wouldn't be surprised if some were trying to weasel in on reward money. If anyone has any question, just ask Amanda Berry: *Who kicked in your door, the Dominican guy or the black guy?* In fact, Cleveland Police detective Andrew Harasimchuk asked Amanda that very question. Here's what he said later, at Ariel's sentencing hearing in August:

"She was able to open the main door of the home, then the storm door. The screen door was locked and she couldn't open it.

"She began banging on the glass and calling for help. At this time a man and a woman from across the street came to Ariel Castro's yard and while there in the yard, a man from next door also came over and was up on the porch and began telling Amanda to kick out the bottom panel of the door."

Case closed.

Within minutes the cavalry came charging down Seymour Avenue, police cars with their lights flying. I stood in the middle of the street, holding my cell phone, flagging them down. I wanted them to see that I was the one who called them; otherwise I feared they probably would have jumped out and cuffed up the street thug–looking black dude—me. I probably shouldn't make that assumption about the Cleveland cops. I'm sure the vast majority are not that way, but I guess after being arrested as many times as I have in the past it just becomes a force of habit. See the police car, get cuffed.

The cops jumped out and ran up to Amanda. She looked very out of place there on Seymour Avenue, kind of the way I would stand out at a Donny and Marie concert. Then Amanda told them, "There's two more in the house!"

What? Wow, this was getting weirder by the moment. Two more still inside? The cops drew their guns and charged in. One female officer stayed outside, consoling Amanda and her still-wailing daughter.

As Michelle Knight would later say on the "Dr. Phil" show, back inside the house she and Gina DeJesus heard a banging sound. They hid because they thought someone was trying to break in.

They were right—those were my foot stomps they heard, trying to break in.

Two cops crawled in through the broken lower panel on the storm door. The second one then kicked the door open so more cops could follow. A few minutes later, Gina and Michelle emerged. Gina was wearing a bright blue sweater and pajama bottoms, and tennis shoes. Michelle was wrapped in a blanket, shaking. All three girls looked rather scrawny.

Meanwhile, the police continued to question Amanda. She told them Ariel had gone off to his mother's house.

"What kind of car does he have?" they asked.

Ariel had a mini-used car lot in his back yard. I looked over there and saw the Jeep Cherokee, the Toyota Tundra, the Harley Davidson, and the Yamaha 900 crotch rocket. I knew which car was missing. "He's in a blue Mazda Miata convertible," I told them.

An ambulance arrived amid all the chaos on the street, and the four girls were helped into the back.

At this point, the swelling crowd began to turn angry. See, one of the girls was Gina DeJesus, a Puerto Rican girl. While this mostly Puerto Rican crowd was joyful to see Amanda and Michelle be freed, it began to turn into a lynch mob when it saw that Gina was among the hostages. The mob was livid that a Puerto Rican dude would do this to a Puerto Rican girl. Had Ariel showed up at this point, the cops would have had one hell of a time keeping the crowd from shredding his fat ass.

Meanwhile, a few blocks away at the McDonald's I had patronized just a few minutes earlier, the cops swooped into the parking lot and surrounded the blue Miata, with the unsuspecting Ariel still inside along with his brother Onil.

I still hadn't yet put together all the pieces. I stood there on the street, talking to the police. They wanted to know every detail of everything I knew. The questioning went on and on. Now the

The front door of Ariel Castro's house was no match for my size 13 shoe.
(EPA/David Maxwell/Landov)

news media trucks and cameras were arriving. The neighbors kept pouring out to see what was happening. Seymour Avenue had turned into Cleveland Mardi Gras.

"Do you know who you just found?" this dude Detective Cook asked me. "That's Amanda Berry. We've been looking for her and those other girls for 10 years."

Ten years? Unfreakin' believable! I'd lived there on Seymour for about a year and had not a flipping clue. Then the math added up in my head. Yeah, I *had* heard the name before. Amanda Berry, the girl who'd been kidnapped something like 10 years ago. The story was big when it broke, but it faded over the years. I thought by this time the girl probably was long dead. *And she had been right next door?*

*   *   *

The police questioning went on for several hours. I stood there in the street. We didn't go down to the station or sit down in my house. Finally, after dealing with all those cops and their questions, the media came looking for me. One word: *crushing*.

Probably the most widely remembered interview I did was with WEWS Channel 5 here in Cleveland. That's the interview that, as of this writing, has nearly 8 million hits on YouTube. I said Ariel must have had "some real big testicles to pull this off." Then I said, "Bro, I knew something was wrong when a little pretty white girl ran into a black man's arms. Something is wrong here. Dead giveaway. Dead giveaway. Dead giveaway. Either she's homeless or she's got problems. That's the only reason why she run to a black man." I mugged for the camera and gave a big thumbs-up.

Okay, I'm stereotyping all over the place here. It's all politically incorrect as can be. I understand that. But I'm just telling you the way of the streets. The mean, twisted streets of drugs, gangs, addiction, despair, and violence. The streets that have been my world. If you don't like it, then put down this book and enjoy the blessings of your four-bedroom split-level there in leafy Rocky River, and God bless you for it. You do and say what you need to do and say to get by in your environment. I do what I need to do in mine. Stereotyping isn't cool for all you well-meaning do-gooder suburbanites. But here in the crumbling concrete jungle it's a survival skill.

Judging by the content of the tsunami of mail and texts I received, virtually no one had a problem with my comment. In fact, they were very supportive. Out of the thousands of cards, letters, and messages, only one guy, some Australian, thought my comment was inappropriate. He probably just got hit in the head with a boomerang one too many times.

A reporter for Channel 8 was caught a bit off-guard at the frankness of my answers. Almost freaked the dude out. After it got posted on YouTube, one viewer wrote, "I've never seen a black

My house is on the left. Ariel's is on the right. Who knew that for all those years those women were just a few feet away? *(EPA/David Maxwell /Landov)*

guy so nervous around another black guy. That reporter is just terrified."

"This dude is the man!! Newscaster looked scared as hell at the end," wrote another viewer.

Across town, at the Louis Stokes VA hospital in Cleveland, the staff kept coming into my father's room. "Mr. Ramsey," they kept saying, one by one, "is that your son on TV? Did you hear what he did?" I'm sure the old man said something to the effect of "Oh, fuck. Now what did that bastard do? Mass murder? Assassination? Ten kilos of cocaine? Shit, I can only imagine." But to his surprise, when he flipped on the TV he saw that despite all those cops and FBI agents around, I wasn't in handcuffs. I actually did something good. (A few weeks later when I made my first visit to him after the rescue, it seemed like every staff member whipped out their cell phone camera and swarmed on me like the paparazzi. It still happens when I go over there to this day.)

On Seymour Avenue the carnival atmosphere continued long into the evening. About an hour after the rescue, while the party was just beginning, one dude recognized another dude as the guy who shot him. They took off down Seymour toward the church and duked it out. But everyone was shaking my hand, congratulating me, high-fiving me, interviewing me, getting their picture with me. It was all good and I'm sure everyone meant well. But after a few hours it was getting to be a bit much. When nobody was looking, I casually ducked away and just started walking.

I headed north up West 25th Street. I figured I'd go hide out at the Riverside Yacht Service, a couple of miles away, down in the flats along the Cuyahoga River. My fellow boarder Shultzie worked there. I thought I could hang with him for a while. I turned up Columbus Road toward the West Side Market, took a right, and ambled down the hill and across the railroad tracks. I walked north on Scranton Road all the way to where it bends around with the river. There, off to the right, finally, was Riverside Yacht Service. But it was gated-up shut, with nasty-ass barbed wire all around. Shit, forget this. I continued my trek until I came back to Columbus, then crossed the river on the drawbridge.

This was a long haul for a 43-year-old man who's been standing around all afternoon. I had no money, and my cell phone was sitting in my living room next to the now cold and slimy Big Mac and limp fries I'd left there hours ago. Yet I trudged on until I saw some bright lights up ahead. It was the Diamond Men's Club on Fall Street. A strip joint—they wouldn't allow TV news cameras in there, so I headed that way.

The hour-long journey had made my feet ache and legs burn as I stopped in front of the club to catch my breath. All those years of smoking and asbestos removal (sometimes not bothering with a respirator) had given me charbroiled lungs. I took a few deep breaths, hands on my knees, and then saw this big guy standing outside the club look at his cell phone, then look at me. This dude looked like he bench-pressed Buicks just because he could, so when he started walking toward me, I wasn't sure what to do. I couldn't run; I was too tired. I would be no match for him if he wanted to rob me, or worse. The dude kept looking at his phone. He walked up to me.

"Hey, man, aren't you the guy who just saved those girls?"

I smiled and nodded, still panting.

"What are you doing here?" he asked.

"Just trying to get away from all them TV cameras," I huffed. "Bad hair day."

"Well, come on in. You can hang out here for a while."

Since this place was open until 2 a.m. and I really had nowhere else to go—I wasn't going back to Seymour—I followed this hulking figure into the club. No cover charge for me. He escorted me through the florescent lighting to the bar, and for the first time in probably eight hours I was able to sit down. I looked up at the six big-screen high-def televisions behind the bar. And there I was. The face that could crack a thousand mirrors. Soon, customers started noticing that the big scary-looking black dude on TV was sitting right among them.

One by one they came over and congratulated me. I heard "God bless you" so many times (a bit ironic to hear in a strip club) that I began to sneeze as if on cue. Every 10 minutes my face and jagged smile were plastered on that TV. The patrons kept cheering me. A few of the ladies who worked there whispered that they would be glad to give me a very special reward. Tempting, yes, but I was just too flippin' tired. I began talking with this Puerto Rican dude, Justo. He goes by Justo Jr. He introduced me to his brothers Wesley and Victor, then pulled out his cell phone and called his uncle.

"Poppy, you won't believe who I'm with right now," he said. "It's that dude on TV. The one who pulled those girls out of that house.

Yeah, he's sitting next to me right now. He needs to get away from all the commotion and shit. I'm bringing him to your house."

With that, Justo Jr. told me to pick myself up and get into his grey BMW X3. The four of us headed out of the flats to I-71 south. We kept driving and driving.

"Where are we headed, bro?" I asked. I was getting a little nervous that maybe I, too, was getting kidnapped.

"To our uncle's house. In Brunswick."

Brunswick? To a street thug from Cleveland, Brunswick was like in Kentucky. Justo Jr. drove down I-71, exited at route 303, and pulled into a ritzy subdivision. No Section 8 housing here. We walked into a spacious house, complete with cathedral ceilings. It was now about 1:30 a.m. The TV was on, and you can guess whose face was on it.

There stood Gino, Justo Jr.'s uncle. "Good shit, Poppy!" he said with a smile. "I'm proud of you. My house is yours." I was exhausted but couldn't sleep. I chilled out as best I could, unaware of the Category 5 hurricane that would strike the next morning. My life was about to go from that of a lowly ex-con, onion-peeling dishwasher to WTF.

MEDIA MADNESS

I wanted to do cartwheels. I know what it's like not to know where your child is. I went through that horrible pain. Here's Charles Ramsey walking home. As he said so succinctly, I'm a black guy. I saw a white woman crying for help, and I went to help her and broke her out. Amanda Berry—saved her life, two other women's lives and that child. And Charles Ramsey is the guy that broke them out of that house of horrors. If I ever meet him I'm going to give him the biggest hug.

—John Walsh
creator of "America's Most Wanted,"
on "ABC's America This Morning."

I TRIED TO CHILL OUT as best I could Monday night. Victor, Justo, Wesley and I camped out in the basement and we watched TV well into the night. There I was on "Piers Morgan." There I was on "Nancy Grace." Finally, at about 5:30, I drifted off. But not for long.

It was maybe 7 a.m. when I was awakened to footsteps bounding down the stairs. One of Gino's sons, Noah, jumped into the bed and pulled out his iPhone and snapped a picture. He wanted to have proof that I actually spent the night at his house. Despite being dog-tired and bleary-eyed, I knew I had to get up. The Cleveland Police wanted me to stop by the Second District headquarters. Also, I wanted to get back to my house and clear things out. I knew that hanging around Seymour Avenue wasn't a good idea. The media circus was one thing, but I felt that some in the neighborhood were none too thrilled with what I had done. I'll discuss more on that later.

I gave Kristen, Gino's wife, my mother's phone number. "I think you should give her a call and tell her I'm OK. While you're at it, maybe you should call my daughter as well." Kristen said that would be no trouble.

The four of us amigos got back in Justo's BMW and headed up north on our way to Seymour Avenue. We stopped at the McDonald's on Bagley Road in Middleburg Heights. I had two sausage breakfast burritos, hash browns, and bottle of Dasani water. The first real meal I had in 24 hours. Justo paid the tab. We pulled onto Seymour Avenue about 9:30 a.m. Hundreds of people and dozens of media trucks clogged the street. The street was barricaded, but when the cops recognized me in the passenger seat they allowed us to pass.

We jumped out of the car and ran into my house to grab the few possessions and clothes I owned. There, sitting in the living room, was my cell phone. I picked it up and couldn't believe what I saw. I had 1,500 missed calls and 3,000 text messages. Before I could mutter "what the . . ." the phone rang. It was my friend Sherman. He had lived in this house before I did.

"Well, well, I'll be damned," Sherman said. "I'll be damned. You've lived there for less than a year and you found those girls. I was there five years and had not a clue. I'll be damned."

The phone rang again. Uruguay.

The phone just kept ringing and ringing. Canada. Russia. China. Bolivia. Israel. England. France. Belgium. Norway. All 50 states. It just wouldn't stop.

We grabbed the rest of my stuff and hopped back in the car, and we rolled down Seymour Avenue.

With my cell phone ceaselessly ringing, and me ignoring same, we headed over to the Cleveland Police Second District headquarters on Clark Avenue. We pulled into the parking lot, and I stepped out. There to greet me were two FBI agents. One was dressed like he came off the cover of GQ. The other guy had a ponytail. They told me they needed me to accompany them back to the FBI building. I got in the back seat of their charcoal grey Ford Taurus and we headed downtown. This made me a bit nervous. Why would these guys want to take me downtown? If they had some questions, they could just ask me at the police station.

One of the agents turned to me as we made our way up West 25th Street. "Wow, you're awesome," he said. "God bless you," the other one said. While I appreciated their kind words, I wasn't sure if it was sincere or if they were trying to soften me up and get me to relax before they sunk their hooks into me.

We arrived at Cleveland FBI headquarters, a sharp-looking brick building on Lakeside Avenue, overlooking Lake Erie. The agents led me up some back steps into an interrogation room. The room was white, simply furnished with a table and four chairs. A red phone hung on the wall. We sat down, and one of them clicked on a microcassette recorder, which seemed odd to me— that a high-tech outfit such as the FBI would still be using such an antique. They had a monitor in front of them and I stared into a camera.

They began to ask questions, pretty much the same questions I'd answered over and over the day before. How well did I know Ariel? How much interaction did I have with him? Were there any clues or indications that there were other people in the house? How often did I see a school bus parked at his house? How well did I know Angel Cordero?

After about 45 minutes, they thanked me for taking the time. Instead of taking me back to Second District headquarters, at my request they dropped me off at Hodge's restaurant on Euclid Avenue. I needed to pick up a paycheck. I texted the other guys in my new posse and told them to meet me there. While I was waiting, the FBI guys came into Hodges and they each ordered a

Ramseyburger, a sandwich the restaurant was serving in my honor. Not only was my paycheck waiting for me, so were two pounds of mail. My co-workers kept saying to me, "You crazy S.O.B!" The rescue was less than 24 hours ago, yet piles of mail had already arrived at Hodges. Justo took a call from his dad and then told me, "We better get back to Brunswick. Anderson Cooper is on a plane and wants to interview you."

Wow. Anderson Cooper! I'd seen Anderson on CNN here and again and I thought he was pretty cool. It's too bad he doesn't like girls because if he did he'd get plenty of 'em without having to pay for any of 'em. Still, I'd be glad to do an interview with him. I'm glad it's him coming out to see me and not some clown like Al Sharpton. I figured Anderson would say something like "I'm here with a human being who saved three other human beings." Al Sharpton would have said something stupid, like "Here's the black guy who saved those white girls." I don't think that way. Yeah, I know Reverend Al said some nice things about me, but I don't care. He even gave me a "patty on the back" for doing all this with a Big Mac in my hand. But it nauseates me how he makes a living convincing us colored folk that we're still slaves and victims of society. One big reason why there's still so much poverty and crime in the black community is because race hustlin', poverty pimpin' con men convince minorities to be victims instead of victors.

Anderson Cooper arrived Tuesday afternoon at Gino's house. Anderson was looking casual but spiffy, wearing a checkered shirt and no tie. He asked if I wanted to do the interview there or if I wanted to do it on Seymour Avenue.

"Ugh. I don't think I should hang around that street. Let's do it here, and if you want to go up there and take a look around then by all means."

We proceeded to do the interview in Gino's spacious backyard.

"You'd seen Ariel around. What was he like?" Anderson asked.

"Cool," I said, matter-of-factly. "He was no freak of nature.

The first 48 hours were non-stop interviews, which I did with hardly any sleep.

He was like me and you. He'd talk about the same thing you talk about, you know what I mean? Regular stuff, bro."

I went on to give the details of the rescue, like I had already done a couple dozen times in the past 24 hours. Wesley and Victor decided to be cute little assholes and photobomb the interview.

"Do you feel like a hero?" Anderson asked.

"No," I said forcefully as lawnmowers buzzed in the background. "No, no, no, no. Bro, I'm a Christian and an American. I'm just like you. We bleed the same blood and put our pants on the same way. It's just that you got to put that being a coward, and 'I don't want to get in nobody's business' away for a minute.

You got to have some cojones, bro. That's all it's about. It's about cojones on this planet."

"Has the FBI said anything about a reward or anything?"

"I'll tell you what you do. Give it to them. Folks who've been following this case since last night, and following me since last night, know I got a job anyway." I then proudly pulled out the paycheck envelope I had picked up a few hours earlier and showed it to Anderson. "What does that address say?" I asked him. Anderson couldn't read it, not having his glasses. I read the address, 2203 Seymour Avenue.

I guess the best line of the interview was the last one. I told Anderson that had I known earlier what was going on in that house, I would have exacted revenge on Ariel in my own way. "Man, I'd be facing triple life," I said. And I meant it.

*   *   *

Gino was acting as point man with the barrage of media inquiries. He told me ABC television wanted me to appear on "Good Morning America" with George Stephanopoulos on Wednesday morning. The interview would be done remotely—George was going to be in New York and I was going to be in a small studio in Independence. I was to go the Ritz-Carlton Hotel downtown that evening and would be picked up in the morning. Justo, Wesley, and Victor joined me, and we drove downtown and checked in. We had the evening free, so we spent some time checking out the Horseshoe Casino. Everywhere I walked, people pointed, came up to me, high-fived me, slapped me on the back. One big black guy came up to me, shook my hand, and wanted to get a picture with me. Sure, I said, not knowing who this big dude was. Later on I found out that was Cleveland Browns defensive back Joe Haden. My entourage and I walked around downtown for a few hours in the night, just to see if the homeless people recognized me. They did.

At 5:30 a.m. I was picked up at the hotel and taken to the studio. I took a seat on the set, which had a photo of the Cleveland skyline as a backdrop. I was so tired and bleary-eyed I could barely stay awake. The only thing keeping me from dropping over unconscious was adrenaline and a can of Red Bull. I put on the earpiece and heard George lead in.

"We are joined now by the man who made this rescue happen, Charles Ramsey. Mr. Ramsey, thank you so much for joining us this morning."

I stared into the camera, my bloodshot eyes drooping under my backward baseball cap.

"I know it has been a whirlwind for you since Monday night. How are you feeling?" George asked.

"I'm happy. You know, I've been pushing to the level as . . . here," I mumbled as I showed the can of Red Bull.

"A little Red Bull helps. OK, I understand that," George said with a laugh, as I let out a huff and took a swig of bottled water.

"Has it sunk in with you?" George asked.

I could only manage to mutter an "uh-uh." I had never been coached on how to properly be interviewed, and I was just plain too tired to care. My eyes wandered around the studio, and I couldn't come up with much more than very simple, quick answers. George asked me if I had any clue that something was going on in Ariel's house.

"Not one iota," I said. "Because I wouldn't have been speaking to this dude. I give this dude his mail when it comes to my house. I eat his food when he feels like barbequing. When he feels like playing salsa music, I try to, you know, merengue. Had I known that, well this would be a whole different interview, now wouldn't it?"

"There was nothing at all in his demeanor that would give you the inkling that he could do something like this?"

"No," I said firmly. "Ain't that scary?"

"It is."

"So either I'm that stupid, or his kind are that good."

That last comment got me into some trouble. What I meant by "his kind" was that he was a monster. It had nothing to do with ethnicity. Comments posted later on YouTube suggested I was high or spaced out. I may have been spaced out, but you would have been too if you'd slept only three of the previous 72 hours.

Then it was off to the studio at WKYC TV3 (right next door to the FBI building) to be interviewed on the set during the noon news. Once again I repeated the story, this time to anchorman Russ Mitchell. The first thing he talked about was my obvious lack of sleep.

"You wanna go to sleep because you know in your heart you've done a good deed," I said, "but since those kids were next door to me, it's hard to sleep."

"Has it sunk in just how much attention you're getting?" Russ asked. "The world is talking about what you did."

"Let me tell you something. I'm an American, and I'm a human being. I'm just like you. I work for a living. There was a woman in distress, so why turn your back on that? My father would have whooped the hell out of me if he found out that I had cowarded out."

After the interview, Wesley told me the ABC people in New York wanted to fly me out there for an interview. My entourage and I would be flown out there first class, and I would be interviewed for ABC's "Nightline" program. The boys and I were excited about the trip—we were going to live like true cool-ass niggas! We went back to Gino's house in Brunswick to get ready. We had to catch an 11 a.m. flight out of Cleveland for Newark, N.J.

My entourage and I arrived at the airport about 10:45 a.m. A golf cart whisked us away to a special TSA holding room. We waited in there until we were carted to the gate. No identification, no metal detector, no getting half-undressed and standing in line. We also had no baggage. None of us. Not a single clean pair of socks among us all. While we were in the holding room, Wesley was monitoring the incoming phone calls. The phone buzzed, and Wesley's eyes got as big as Ariel's testicles.

"It's the White House!" he shouted. "The goddamn White House is calling."

Wesley carefully put the phone on a table. Everyone, including all the TSA people, gathered around with hushed anticipation. I gingerly pushed the green button and put the phone on speaker.

"Hello?" I said softly. We all knew what voice we were about to hear.

"Mr. Ramsey?"

"Yes, right here, sir."

"Mr. Ramsey, this is Secretary—." He gave his name, but I can't remember it.

"Wha? Dis ain't Barack?"

"No, I'm a cabinet secretary. I work very closely with the president. On behalf of the United States government, I want to commend you for your quick action and heroic deed. Congratulations, sir."

Pause. "Dis ain't Barack?"

"No, Mr. Ramsey. The president has seen on the news what you did. He's very grateful for what you did for those girls."

"Uh, thanks. Just did what I had to do, bro." The group let out a collective sigh of disappointment. I guess it's still an honor to be called by a cabinet secretary, and it probably was a good thing that it wasn't Barack calling me. Trust me, I would have had a few things to say to him. He would have wound up hanging up on me, and for sure my ass would have been audited.

When we arrived in Newark, we were picked up in a cool-ass black Lincoln Navigator, complete with tinted windows, that was going to take us across the river to a cool-ass Hyatt Regency Hotel.

"Oh, you're amazing," the driver said. "I have daughters. What you did makes me want to cry."

I probably heard that a few dozen times over the first few days.

Of course my phone kept ringing and ringing, but I had Wesley monitor it. While on the way to the hotel, a certain name kept popping up on the caller ID over and over.

"Hey Chuck," Wesley said excitedly. "The caller ID says Snoop Dogg!"

"Yeah, like hell it is," I said. Yeah, sure, Snoop Dogg is among the thousands of people trying to get ahold of me. Some schmuck was putting that in his caller ID to trick me into answering. You're not going to fool this cool-ass nigga.

But the phone kept buzzing with Snoop Dogg showing up on the caller ID. So finally I told Wesley, "Tell that mothafucka to text me his picture. If he won't do it or it's not *the* Snoop Dogg, then tell him to go play with his mother."

Sure enough, Wesley told the caller to text a picture. There was Snoop Dogg's picture. I told Wesley to go ahead and call the number back.

"Hello, is this Mr. Ramsey?" Snoop asked Wesley.

"Yeah, this is his representative, calling back."

"Whadup, this is Snoop Dogg. I'm tryin' to highlight him, man. We love what he did, man. He's a hero around my way."

"Hey hey hey, we love him too. You know what, Snoop? I've been denying everyone's phone calls, but because it's you calling I'ma let you get a couple seconds with him right now because he hasn't slept in four days since the incident happened. You know he hasn't had no rest. But since it's you calling I'ma let you get on the phone real fast."

Wesley handed the phone to me. "It's Snoop Dogg. Snoop Doggy Dog."

I snatched the phone out of Wesley's hand. "Snoop? Get the fuck outta here!"

"Mr. Ramsey, it's me baby. Wassup wit ya, brudder? I just wanna commend you for your great work. You're a hero."

"Oh my God," I said in disbelief. "What's crackalackin' cuz?" I had a specific reason for using the word "crackalackin." Snoop was a Crip, so you use words with "c." You do all you can to avoid words that begin with "b," since that was the first letter for Bloods, the Crips' sworn enemy.

"I'm chillin' with a friend of mine," Snoop said. "I just want you to know you're a hero, man. That was some great, great shit you did, man, and you should be commended for that."

"No, no. Come on, Mr. Broadus, you would have done the same thing, bruh, you know how we cut. You'd a done the same thing, my nigga. It ain't about no fuckin' hero. Couldn't let that girl stay up in that crib no mo, bro."

"Now you did that. Now hopefully we can make the shit aware so that someone else can get found along the way because that was some great shit you did."

While we were having this conversation, I was with my boys chillin' in the back of the Lincoln Navigator that ABC had provided us. And I thought Snoop was just chillin' in his crib. I had no idea this was a live interview for an Internet broadcast on the GGN Hood News Network. Otherwise I wouldn't have said the stupid shit I said next. I went off on Angel Cordero, telling Snoop Dogg that I wanted him to come to Cleveland and help me beat the shit out of Angel.

"This mothafuckin' Dominican, on the fuckin' news, talking about what the fuck *he* done did and how *he* helped *me* do something. Hey—if you could just watch my back while I beat the fuck out this nigga when I get back to Cleveland. I think it'd look real good if Snoop watch me beat this so-called hero up."

"I got your back, loved one. You just let me know when and where to be."

Now, I have no desire to go beat anybody up. I just said that out of frustration because I had seen reports on the news questioning my truthfulness on how this whole thing went down. I had no idea my words were going to be broadcast anywhere. It was a *dumb* thing to say. But hey, after going on four days with almost no sleep it was plenty easy to say something dumb.

We arrived at the Hyatt Regency and checked in. A fancy joint crawling with Caucasians, except for the help. I noticed the room rate—$517 a night. We got two adjoining rooms, which we combined into one by opening the pass-through door. Now I was getting a taste of how a cool-ass nigga lives. And I didn't have to sell any crack or pimp out any pain-in-the-ass whiny crack whores. I flicked on the TV. There I was, again.

"Shit, this is turning out to be more of a big fuckin' deal than I thought," I told the boys.

Even though the Hyatt was a five-star hotel, just across the street were the projects. What a contrast, but that's what you find all throughout New York.

Around 4 p.m. we left the hotel for Flatbush, a community in Brooklyn, where Gino's sister lived in a two-bedroom apartment. She cooked us some beef empanadas with Spanish rice. Good Puerto Rican shit. We chilled out, watched more TV, and played cards. Gino's sister kept sobbing for joy every time I showed up on the news. We got back to the Hyatt about midnight. For the first time since the rescue, I actually got a decent night's sleep. The next afternoon I was going to be interviewed by Cynthia McFadden for ABC's "Nightline."

Meanwhile, back at Hodge's, "Nightline" interviewed Peter Brooks, a manager there at the restaurant.

"All I can say is the phone here is non-stop ringing," Pete said.

"They are doing T-shirts. There are people calling to donate money. There are women calling to ask him if he's married."

Yeah, I'm every woman's dream. My track record with women isn't very good. If I married you, I'd probably run up your debt, mess up your credit, take what I wanted, then leave you. Oh, yea, I'd probably sleep with your sister, too.

The next morning we got up and out to see the sights. I wasn't getting paid a nickel for this interview, and we didn't have much expense money. Room service was not part of the deal. I told the driver that I wanted to see all five boroughs in the five hours we had until I had to be at the ABC studios. That's a near-impossible task since it can take an hour just to drive through some sections without even taking time to look around. Still, we drove all around, and I rolled down the tinted window and waved at the people. Many of them recognized me, and I heard many more "God bless yous" and the like. Many came up to shake my hand and get my picture. Hell, even some damn homeless people came up and gave me money.

I didn't want to see just the glamorous parts of the city. I wanted to see where the city never sleeps. I wanted to see the projects, the scummy parts, where the drug dealers work the mean and tangled streets. Our driver was either too scared or just knew better. "Not on this trip," he said.

Before we made our way to the studios, we stopped at a McDonald's. I got a Big Mac, and as I arrived at the ABC studios I walked in there with the sandwich in hand, just for a joke. They miked me up and readied me for the interview.

Dan Harris, the anchor, opened with, "There is no résumé, no formula for heroism. Sometimes it is the most unlikely people who step up. Such was the case in Cleveland this week when a very idiosyncratic hero emerged to help put to an end to one of the most horrific kidnapping cases in memory. His name is Charles

Ramsey. He is a dishwasher-turned-icon who has a special way with words, as 'Nightline' anchor Cynthia McFadden learned first-hand."

Idiosyncratic? What's with all these smooth damn Caucasian words? If I'd written that script, it would have been direct and to the point, something like, "Here's Chucky, that toothless nigga who found them girls."

I turned on the charm with Cynthia. She was wearing a bright blue blazer, and I was dressed in all black with my signature Cleveland Indians baseball cap backward on my nappy head.

We talked about how my phone had been blowing up since the rescue. She scrolled through the incoming texts and calls.

"There are numbers in this phone," I said, "that start off with 9456500000 hyphen sumthin' sumthin' sumthin' hyphen, so I'm just guessing that's Denmark." I shrugged my shoulders. "I ain't got no friends with no numbers with hyphens. I don't even have friends that can spell the word 'hyphen.'"

Cynthia kept scrolling through all the texts.

"You're a hero, man. Greetings from Malaysia," she read as she took off her glasses and started nibbling on one end, which made me squirm a bit in delight. "What does that feel like, Charles?"

"That feels like Boost Mobile is going to charge me more than $50 a month. It feels like I messed up that unlimited plan dramatically."

I couldn't resist calling Cynthia "Sugah" a couple of times. I stared at her right in the eyes and mesmerized her. Of course, some wise ass there at ABC had seen the story about my criminal record on Channel 5 back in Cleveland or online on thesmokinggun.com, and Cynthia brought it up, mentioning my conviction on domestic violence charges resulting from an incident with my wife Rochelle in 2003. I just told the unvarnished truth. "I was a piece of shit. She deserved better."

At the end of the interview I said, "When you reach that age, it's like, I am going to be a total schmuck the rest of my life, or are we going to stop being a schmuck?"

Cynthia replied, "Well on Monday, you showed the world you weren't a schmuck."

"Don't know about next Monday. Can't promise you nuthin'," I said with a wink.

Cynthia extended her hand, and I took it and kissed it. I'm sure she ran to the ladies' room and scrubbed it to the bone the moment I left.

Afterward, people apparently bombarded Channel 5 with negative reaction for putting out the story of my past. Channel 5 apologized for dredging up my criminal record. They posted on Facebook:

"TO OUR READERS & FOLLOWERS: We heard you. Wednesday night, we made a poor judgment call in posting a story about Charles Ramsey's criminal record and how he's since reformed. While the story was factually sound, the timing of it and publication of such information was not in good taste, and we regret it. Your comments prompted us to quickly remove the story from our website and Facebook page, but we know we can't erase what we've already done. Ramsey is a hero for his actions, and we recognize that. Thank you so much for your feedback."

I'm not pissed at anyone at Channel 5. They were just doing their job. The reaction across this goddamn planet had been so overwhelmingly positive that it would have taken a video of me kicking fuckin' crippled puppies to have any serious negative impact. The hundreds of comments and thousands of "likes" on Channel 5's Facebook post reflected that.

Even my ex-wife, Rochelle, said some nice things about me. She posted on her Facebook page, "For the record, people do change and you shouldn't hold the past against someone. The main thing is that Charles Ramsey did a good deed and those girls are safe. Is that not the most important thing?" That was indeed an awfully nice thing to say about someone who tried to kill her. That's how fucked up this crack dealer was back then. I'll tell you about it later, but I was more than a piece of shit. I was the whole steamy, runny pile.

Back in the ABC studio, after the "Nightline" interview was over, the boys and I gathered ourselves together and headed out to the lobby. We found the driver and told him we were ready to go to the airport.

"Oh," he said. "You've got your plane tickets?"

"Uh, no," I said. "We figured you'd have 'em for us here."

"No. We don't have any tickets for you."

"What the fuck?" I yelled. "Whaddaya mean you don't got no fuckin' tickets? How the fuck are we supposed to get back home?"

"Sorry, we don't have any tickets for your return trip."

I whipped out my phone and called Gino.

"Poppy, these muthafuckas are tryin' to tell us they got no goddamn airplane tickets to get us home."

"You stupid shits," Gino bellowed back at me. "I tried to tell you. When ABC offered to fly you assholes out there, they made it clear that those tickets were one-way only. Once the interview was done, they were done with your black and brown asses. But you fuckers thought you were all hot-shit niggas and thought they'd kiss your asses all the way back to Cleveland. This is what happens when you don't listen to me." Gino roared on and on, lapsing into a string of Spanish obscenities.

"Ah, shit, Poppy," I said. "So now what the fuck are we supposed to do?"

"Give me a couple hours, dumbfuck. I'll make some phone calls and see what I can do."

If anyone could figure out how to get our asses out of this sling, it would be Gino. I had a good idea—if ABC didn't find a way to get us back home, we'd walk over to the CBS studios and tell them just how the muthafuckas at ABC treat their guests.

Of course the phone just kept ringing and ringing and ringing. Finally, Wesley saw it was Gino calling. He had indeed fixed the problem, and the people at ABC would take us to the airport. We had confirmation numbers and everything. After I hit the end call button, I took that goddamn phone and threw it as long and as far as I could. It splashed into the Hudson River, where it remains in its silent watery grave to this day. When the phone bill for May arrived, the final totals were in: 257 outgoing text messages; 60,000 incoming.

*   *   *

With our ticket crisis resolved, we were driven back across the river to Newark Airport. We got dropped off, but this time we had to go through the regular security line. One problem: I had no ID. I had no car, and thus no need for a driver's license. So when I got to the TSA agent checking IDs, I explained I didn't have one. The agent said I would have to go into a room where they could do some additional screening. The rest of my posse had IDs, so they made it through no problem.

I was taken to a side room where they began asking all these questions. I was a bit ticked, because I had no problem getting here with no ID, so why the big deal to let me get back home?

I started going apeshit. "Haven't you seen this fuckin' face on your TV for four days straight?" I asked incredulously.

Other people in the room saw and heard what was going on, and a few pulled out their cell-phone cameras.

"Back in Cleveland no one asked for an ID or anything," I said.

"Sorry, sir. We have to follow standard policy."

They made phone calls to the Division of Motor Vehicles in

Columbus, and to Social Security. They had to see if my name matched up with the Social Security number I was providing, and also verify my mother's maiden name.

Finally they finished their shit, and I headed for the gate. As I walked through the airport, again the crowds gathered. The usual platitudes, but it was fun. As we got on the plane, the pilot greeted me at the door.

"You're the guy who found those girls!" he said, repeating the line I've heard a thousand times before and after. "Come on in here, sit down!" The pilot stepped back and pointed me to the cockpit. I'm sure it violated all sorts of Homeland Security laws, but I put my ass in the pilot's seat. Damn, I looked good in it. After a minute of chillin' with the crew, I headed back to my seat, to the cheers of those on board.

When we arrived in Cleveland, Gino was there to greet us. He was still scowling, and still had plenty of names to call us as we drove back to Brunswick.

When we arrived at the house, Kristen told me I better call my mother. By the way she said it, I knew it couldn't be good.

"Hey, Mom. It's me." I hadn't spoken to her in about seven months. Not that I had any great animosity toward her; it's just that she lived in Alabama and I just didn't care one way or another what was going on in her life. She's a Jehovah's Witness, so when she's not home she's out bothering others.

"Oh my, it's you," she said. "You've been on TV nonstop since yesterday afternoon. Well, I must say I'm not the least bit surprised. I always knew you had it in you to do something good. I'm just glad as can be that I'm seeing you did something so big and it didn't land you in jail."

"Yeah, well, I just did what I had to do," I said.

Then she tore into me.

"But just why did you tell that Snoopy Dogg character on TV

that you were going to beat up some Dominican, you stupid dumb nigga? Why would you say something like that to embarrass this family? I still got church friends up there, you know. I raised you to be a Christian, and you know better than that. Who taught you to cuss like that? And just who the hell is this Snoopy Dogg?"

I was stunned. Not because my mother just ripped me a new asshole—she's done that a few dozen times—but because this is when I found out that my conversation with Snoop Dogg had been broadcast. Remember, I thought Snoop had been calling me from his fuckin' living room, not for broadcast on some network. Apparently some TV station had picked up on it and broadcast some of my comments.

The dust from this furor had hardly started to settle when Gino told me something else that blew me away.

"Some idiot is on TV impersonating you," he said.

Turns out that someone had tricked the producers of the TMZ TV show, convincing them that that he was really me! TMZ ran with the story but then pulled it after a call from a lawyer who was voluntarily helping me out.

"A crew from '60 Minutes' Australia wants to do an interview with you," Gino said. Gino had made arrangements for me to stay at the Marriott on West 150th at I-71. "They'll meet with you tomorrow in the lobby," he told me.

*   *   *

I got a call to appear on the "Rock Newman Show," a talk radio show in Washington, D.C. Rock is quite an accomplished character, from baseball all-American at Howard University to super salesman to sports agent to talk-show host. He's interviewed and/ or met with the pope, Nelson Mandela, assorted presidents and movie stars, but that was just the undercard. Now he was going to interview me.

After the near disaster in New York, Gino came along to keep an eye on us. We arrived at the airport in D.C. on Friday afternoon and were picked up in Rock's white Rolls-Royce Phantom. We saw some of the sights around town. I particularly enjoyed touring the *Sequoia*, the presidential yacht. It was mind-blowing. I saw where President Kennedy had his last birthday party, the spot where President Truman banged his cigar cutter on the dining-room table, and I held an impromptu mini press conference while lying across the bed where President Kennedy banged Marilyn Monroe.

We then had dinner at a bordello-red burlesque place and hung around at a gentleman's club. We were supposed to stay at some fancy hotel, but I never made it up to the room. After the club, Wesley and I went on to a restaurant. Some black dude dishwashers recognized me and came out and invited us to hang around with them.

Later that night Wesley and I got bored, so we decided to try to get robbed. We walked around the streets of D.C. with $20 bills hanging from our pockets. We would pull out our cell phones and say, "Damn, no signal here, and it looks like we're LOST." The plan was to get someone to try to rob us, and then I was going to be a hero again. Unfortunately, or fortunately, the streets of D.C. were just too damn safe that night, so we never got a chance to bust up a robbery. I know, it was one dumb-fuck idea, but, hey, we were two bored kids.

We stayed out till 7 a.m., when my phone rang. Gino had noticed we weren't at the hotel, and we had to be at the studio soon for the 9 a.m. show.

"Where the fuck are you assholes NOW?" Gino yelled. "Get your goddamn asses back here; we got a show to do."

We made it in time to be picked up and driven from the hotel to the storefront studio of WPWC Radio 1480 in the Anacostia neighborhood of D.C. I stepped out of the Phantom and was in front of Ben's Chili Bowl when someone came up to me and shouted, "You're, like, a lifesaver. I've been watching this on the news all the time and here you are! Facebook material!" As soon as that guy shot a picture, a D.C. cop on a Segway rolled up and wanted to get a picture with me.

The studio was in Washington; the broadcast area was centered in southern Prince George's County, Va., on a 5,000-watt station. The show was also televised online.

Before a live studio audience, the broadcast bumped in with the Sly and the Family Stone tune "Everyday People." Rock said, "Today is a very special and historic day for the 'Rock Newman Show' . . ." He started at the very beginning and asked about my childhood, things I remembered from way back when, and things I did in school. He spent a fair amount of time talking about my domestic violence conviction, although emphasizing that it was so far in the past it didn't matter anymore. Having been up all fuckin' night, I stumbled a bit on my words and left some dead air space between questions during the first half of the show, but as we continued I warmed up, especially when we got into the details of the rescue.

The biggest reaction from the audience came when Rock asked me about my celebrity status, and I responded with, "Amanda Berry—that's the damn celebrity, not me. I just played my position." I really mean that. Think about it—what I did was a reaction to a dramatic situation. Yes, I took a risk, but Amanda took a much bigger risk. When she started banging on that door, she didn't know if anyone would help her. Had she not gotten out and had Ariel then come home, damn, the consequences would have been brutal at best. That fucker would have fucked her up something fierce.

"If I have something that I could say to my fellow media folks out there," Rock said, wrapping up the 90-minute interview, "understand and recognize this man for who he is and the heroic act that he has taken. He honest-to-God did something that exemplifies in the very best of us that which we want to be. He was brave and courageous in the time of difficulty and adversity."

Thanks, Rock. That's a very nice thing to say to an ex-con, ex-drug dealin', ex-wife beatin', ex-jail-breakin' (oh yeah, that's on my résumé, too—stay tuned) . . . But like I said, I just played my position and reacted on instinct. It's those girls who went through unbelievable difficulty and adversity.

*   *   *

I had no real advisors, publicists, or public relations people. Just a few people who tried to help, and a few who tried to hitch on for the ride.

Out of the blue, a successful disability lawyer in Kentucky called me and asked if I'd do a commercial for his law firm. He made arrangements to fly me and my entourage to Kentucky where they held a small press conference and shot the commercial. They unveiled a bust they'd had made of me. I got to take it home. I think it would look good in Mayor Jackson's office.

Anyway, this was in the mountains of Kentucky, where black folks like me and Puerto Ricans like Justo and Wesley are seen only on television. But the good ol' mountain folk were very kind to us, and showed us a good time. We stayed at a huge mansion that resembled Robert Downey Jr.'s digs in the "Iron Man" movies. The ceiling was so fucking high I couldn't hit it with a basketball. Believe me, I tried. It took a hefty Frisbee throw to finally hit the ceiling. We rode around town in a Black S550 Mercedes Benz.

That night, when Victor and I were looking around on the computer to find some local Kentucky women, we Googled up the lawyer's name. Seems he had some serious legal issues of his own. He was being investigated by the feds for his firm's assembly-line style of disability claims. Oh well. I had my certified check for $10,000 and plane ticket for home the next day. That's a problem for the lawyer and all those Caucasian mountain men to figure out.

Other people started using my face and words in all kinds of products. T-shirts, of course, a lot of them, but you could also buy a travel coffee mug with my mug on it, even a fucking iPhone cover. Who the hell would want my face on their iPhone all day long? Some Korean company made a really bad computer video game called "Charles Ramsey's Burger Bash" where you throw hamburgers at Ariel. None of these people asked my permission or offered to pay me anything.

There was a lot of stuff posted on the Internet. Some of it was making me out to be a hero, like a Photoshopped "Man of Steel" movie poster with my face in place of Superman's. But most of it was humorous.

Probably the best known is the "Dead Giveaway" autotuned video on You Tube, put together by the Gregory Brothers. I first came across it while looking around on the Internet. I thought it was hilarious. I sent the Gregory Brothers an email thanking them, and they responded that they were trying to locate me. These guys had created several autotuned videos that went viral. They did a series of videos known as "Songify the News," which included the Bed Intruder song featuring a guy named Antoine Dodson, which got something like 100 million views. They were very gracious in dealing with me and agreed to pay me residuals on the now-famous video they did of me and a song download version. The video's funny, but everyone listen: I'm not a rap star or a singer of any kind. So please don't ask me to sing it—you'll be sorely disappointed.

*   *   *

For weeks and months, cards and letters and texts kept pouring in by the thousands from around the world. There were some cash donations amid the cards and letters, but while some folks seem to think I became some sort of instant millionaire from all the attention, that was definitely not the case.

I traveleled a little, including a trip to Milwaukee in July, where Bone Thugs-N-Harmony brought me up on stage during a show. I got to meet some interesting people. In August I attended a Lil Wayne concert at Blossom Music Center near Cleveland. No sooner had I sat down in the pavilion than an usher tapped me on the shoulder. "Mr. Ramsey, Mr. Wayne would like to meet you backstage." With that, I was escorted behind the curtain and watched the show from backstage. After the show, Lil Wayne came up to me, voice trembling, saying, "That was so beautiful what you did. I want you to come to New Orleans to meet my family."

And I did have the cash to buy a used car, thanks to the Australian TV interview. I bought Justo's 2008 BMW X3 for $8,000. It was great to finally have a car, but I had a little problem: My license had been suspended for about 10 years. I owed some back child support and had a couple of traffic tickets that I never bothered to go to court for. (Hell, if my ass wasn't in jail, it just wasn't important to me.) A suspended license had never kept me from driving, of course. Well, I paid up my support and paid off the tickets—including a $345 ticket for jaywalking.

THE BEGINNINGS

Family is conflict and it's something that we all relate to.
—Bill Cosby

I WASN'T PREPARED FOR THE frenzy that followed the rescue. How could anyone have been ready for that 10-ring circus? But the first 43 years of my life definitely weren't spent grooming myself for the public eye.

It would be easy to blame it all on the dysfunctional relationship I had with my parents. Dad and I got along about as well as a couple of barnyard roosters. But as long as I can remember, I had to do things my way. That got me into trouble over and over again. What should have been a comfortable, upper-class suburban upbringing turned into a chaotic path of delinquency, stupidity, pretty crime, serious crime, drugs, prison—not exactly the things that prepare you for instant international celebrity. I always managed to find drama, but on May 6 the drama found me. Yet, when you look back, it all makes sense in a bizarre sort of way. There has never been a state of "normalcy" in my life. Looking back, I see how the jagged pieces of my life were jammed together, by my parents, teachers, friends, and most of all myself.

*   *   *

My father, Charles Ramsey Sr., was born in the sawmill town of Pine Apple, Alabama, in 1937. In Pine Apple, you either worked at the lumberyard or picked cotton. Those were the only two lines of work available in that part of the country during the Great Depression.

Dad's father worked at the lumberyard as a lumber checker. It was his job to account for every piece of lumber that was being shipped out. One problem: My grandfather never went to school—ever—and thus didn't know how to count. Fortunately he had a white friend who taught him how to count, and, eventually, how to multiply. What my grandfather lacked in knowledge he made up with hard work and grit. He had a nephew, Willie Ramsey, who worked for Daugherty Lumber in the faraway city of Wickliffe, Ohio. Willie put in a good word about my grandfather, and in 1954 the family packed up and moved to Cleveland.

Dad, who was 17 at the time, drove the car. This was before the days of interstate highways, so it was a slow drive through the country roads of the Deep South. At one gas and grocery, they stopped for some gas. Dad went into the store for some milk for his younger sister and promptly got a taste of the darker side of the white Southern hospitality of the times. "You can't buy that," they told him, directing him back to the door. Dad continued on his way, and after a few long, grueling days the Ramseys made it to Cleveland, where they moved into a two-bedroom apartment with two other cousins and their families.

Dad was assigned to East High School, which was 99 percent white at the time. He was enrolled in the 10th grade, but after meeting with a couple of administrators and taking a couple of tests, he was moved up to the 11th grade. Dad had an advantage. Back in Alabama, one of his grandmothers owned a large house and rented several rooms to local elementary school teachers. Being surrounded by teachers, Dad learned to read at an early age, could spell very well, and was well ahead of the other kids, and in fact well ahead of many of their parents, when he started school.

At age 7, I may have been cute, but I was always looking for trouble, usually finding it with ease. *(Charles Ramsey collection.)*

Even though he was smart enough to go to college, Dad chose to enlist in the Air Force after graduating from East High.

After three and a half years stationed in France, Dad came back to Cleveland and became a street hustler in the St. Clair/Lexington/Hough/East 55th area of Cleveland. Dad's specialties—picked up while in the Air Force—were cards and gambling. He became an expert at sleight of hand and dealing off the bottom of the deck. Dad's first exposure to gambling came when his father set up what was known as a "juke joint." Simply, that's what illegal gambling establishments were called. Dad sold drinks from a pop stand in the juke joint while his dad ran the business by cutting the card games and shooting dirty dice. In 1966, Dad was present while another street hustler named Don King stomped the shit out of Sam Garrett, an employee who owed him $600. That was the second dude Don King killed.

Dad then lived for a while in Hempstead, New York, on Long Island, and when Chrysler Corporation announced it was moving its stamping plant from Detroit to Twinsburg, Ohio, Dad drove his cousin to Twinsburg to apply for a job. While waiting for his cousin to be interviewed, one of the supervisors handed Dad an application. Dad said he wasn't there to apply; he was just waiting on his cousin. But the supervisor encouraged Dad to fill out an application anyway, so Dad did. When he got back to New York, he received a telegram to come back to Twinsburg. When he got back, he interviewed and Chrysler offered him a job as long as he could start right away. Dad didn't bother retrieving his clothes or belongings in New York. By the way, his cousin wasn't offered a job.

Married to his first wife, Dad and his family became the first black family to move into the area of East 124th Street and St. Clair. Ten blocks over, another black family moved in—the family of George Forbes, who soon after ran for Cleveland City Council and won. Like George, Dad was a leader of the pack, and George sought Dad out for support. The first person George lined up for a city job was his brother. The second person was Dad. Dad became a draftsman in the civil engineering department, and he continued to work for the city, eventually becoming commissioner of urban development and housing until his retirement in 1988.

Dad and his first wife eventually divorced, and he married my mother in 1968. On September 7, 1969, I was the first-born son to Charles Ramsey Sr. and Maratha Townsend Ramsey in Warrensville Heights, Ohio, at Brentwood Hospital, just to the southeast of Cleveland.

Our family started off in an apartment on Northfield Road. Dad, of course, worked for the city of Cleveland, and my mother would later on work for the Ohio Lottery. My parents bought a house in Cleveland on Hollyhill Drive, off Lee Road between Harvard and Miles, in 1973. With the arrival of my younger brother, Kevin, they bought a five-bedroom house at 15110 Judson Drive through a Veterans Administration foreclosure sale in 1976. (I experienced some sibling jealousy when Kevin was brought home. I liked the being the center of attention.)

When the Cleveland school district was ordered to institute system-wide forced busing, Dad knew what would happen—a mighty school district was going to crumble. He wanted nothing to do with that. Besides, I was already turning into a bit of a troublemaker, and busing me off to some other school farther away would make it harder to keep an eye on me. So in November of 1978 we moved to a three-bedroom house in Richmond Heights. Their house on Judson sold in 1979 for $42,000. Dad paid $155,000 for a slightly larger, but much nicer, home on Donald Drive, near Richmond Mall.

*   *   *

Over the years we made several trips to Alabama. My grandfather liked to go out on his small boat, so one day he hitched the trailer and boat to the back of the car and went to a local lake. I was 13 or 14, so my grandfather trusted me with the important job of holding the rope so the boat wouldn't float away while he launched it from the trailer. I wasn't sure if I was strong enough, so I decided to wrap the rope around my neck so I could use my whole body weight. Common sense tells you that I should have wrapped it around my waist, but common sense was never a strong point of mine. My grandfather launched the boat, and the current began to pull it away. I had no idea just how much force that was going to create on the rope. The next thing I knew, I felt the rope tighten around my neck. Shit! This was the Deep South, and it felt like the Klan had found me. I tried to yell for help, but I couldn't. I hacked and acked like Bill the Cat. The boat floated farther away, and I turned purple. Problem is, it's awfully hard to notice when a black kid's face turns purple. I hit the ground and flopped around like a fish, trying to get the rope off my neck. Finally my grandfather grabbed the rope, yanked the boat back a few feet, and pulled the rope off me.

"You stupid nigga," he said, so matter-of-factly.

*   *   *

I attended Ridgebury Elementary School in Lyndhurst. I was still a wide-eyed innocent tyke when I started school. I remember my first day of school—I proudly wore my Buster Brown shoes, and Mom packed a pickle loaf sandwich and a bag of Fritos in my lunch. Mom was crazy about those brown shoes, but personally I would have preferred a pair of Converse high-tops, like Dr. J wore. After school, we went to Sea World, where I tried to feed some of the Fritos to Shamu. Ever since I can remember, I've always enjoyed entertaining the crowd.

Every chance I could, I would get up in front of the class and tell jokes, make fun of teachers, or just be generally obnoxious—as long as it got a laugh. One time the teacher got so sick of my antics that she locked me in a broom closet all damn day, checking on me every 10 or 15 minutes. Then she told Dad exactly what she did. Dad, of course, thought I deserved that and a whole lot more. Can you imagine the outrage nowadays if a teacher would do something like that? My, have times changed.

At home, I would hear music by the Supremes, the Temptations, the O'Jays, Captain and Tennille, Sonny and Cher and Aretha Franklin. Mom liked to watch "The Dinah Shore Show" and "The

Merv Griffin Show." I enjoyed watching "The Little Rascals," "The Three Stooges," "Scooby-Doo," "Fantasy Island," "Speed Racer," and old Tarzan movies. Dad liked to watch golf, "Meet the Press," golf, Dick Feagler, more golf. Dad really liked Dick Feagler, saying it was because Dick "was from Cleveland, smart, and white."

Even in the 1990s, when I was well into my 20s, Dad made me watch "The Cosby Show" every week. Every Thursday at 8 p.m., Dad flicked it on and ordered me to sit down. Dad never laughed at any of Cosby's jokes or any of the cute things the Huxtable kids said or did, but he had a specific reason for sitting me down to watch that show. Whenever Theo Huxtable got into trouble, Dad would glower at me. Theo would always get these harebrained ideas of how to make fast money or beat the system, and he would always wind up in deep shit until Bill Cosby came along and bailed his ass out, and Theo would realize he wasn't the smartest nigga in the house. That was my recurring pattern of behavior as well, and Dad wanted me to learn from Theo's fuckups.

By the time I was in the fourth grade, all those Captain and Tennille songs messed up my head so bad and caused me to get into trouble so many times that my mother took me to see a psychiatrist. But there was nothing wrong with me, the psychiatrist lady concluded. And she was right. I knew exactly what I was doing. It was fun to cause trouble and be disruptive. One time I took a standard No. 2 pencil, nice and freshly sharpened, and balanced it upright on a chair belonging to a girl who sat next to me. She didn't see it and sat straight on it.

"Yeowwwww!" she screamed, with tears running down her face. But I actually found that to be funny. I know, it was a horrible thing to do. But to me school was boring and uninteresting. The poor girl had to go to the hospital, and I got into a fuckload of trouble, but it was worth it. This was my type of entertainment.

I can't begin to estimate the number of times Mom got a call from school about my behavior. She'd just shake her head and hang up the phone and then beat the shit out of me. Eventually it got to the point where she just took the call, listened to the teacher, and hung up. She no longer gave a damn about what I got into and didn't want to expend the energy it would take to wallop me.

After elementary school, I attended Memorial Junior High in South Euclid. My objective was simple: become a full-time asshole. Not in a mean way, but in a how-can-I-fuck-things-up-today manner. And I was very good at it. I cut classes every day, and every teacher of course was a moron. My mother saw the horror movie "Child's Play," about an out-of-control doll named Chucky, which convinced her that she'd given me the right nickname. She also saw the movie "The Omen" and subsequently refused to ever get us a dog. These are reasons why every May I go into the local copy shop, drop my pants, sit on the photocopier, and make a heartfelt Mother's Day card from the bottom of my black ass.

I wish I could say I had a Beaver and Wally relationship with my parents, but that is just not true. Dad was a tyrant in every way. Physically, mentally, psychologically, you name it, he was and still is a controlling bastard through and through. Yes, he put a roof over our heads and we weren't wanting for money, but that was it: Money was dad's method of trying to control people. He wasn't generous. He used money to get his way, always. If he spent money on you, he felt entitled to tell you exactly what you could and couldn't do. While it's true he spent a lot of money on me, it was because he was trying to control every aspect of my life, including trying to keep me away.

Just recently he was transferred from a VA hospital to a nursing home, much to the relief of the staff at the hospital. He lingers on to this day, rotting of cancer, and no one in the family gives a shit. After the way he treated everyone, no one, including me, cares if he just slowly rots away.

Oh come on, Chuck, you say. *Forgive and make peace with your dad in his final days.* Ok, the bastard's forgiven, but the best way for me to make peace with him is to stay the hell away. Even if I had been the perfect son, he still would have been the perfect asshole. Somehow my mother, who has a few loose screws to begin with, stayed with him for over 35 years. She joined the Jehovah's Witnesses in the early '90s so she could spend her free time away from the house bothering others, which she found to be a much more enjoyable alternative than being home putting up with his shit. We had always been members of Everlasting Missionary Baptist Church at the corner of Eddy and St. Clair. Dad declared that we were born and raised Baptist and will always be Baptists. Anything that strayed from the Baptist line was sheer apostasy. Finally she had enough and they divorced in 2006. Mom then moved back to Alabama.

Here's an example of what a sick bastard Dad was. He had somehow convinced his parents that he and he alone should be the sole heir of their estate. Dad had a brother and a sister, who lived in their parents' free-and-clear home on St. Clair Avenue. Living with them were his sister's two young children. After my grandmother died, Dad took title to the property, and one day a for-sale sign showed up in the front yard. Dad didn't say anything to them about selling the house. The sign just showed up one morning, and Dad told his brother and sister to be out in 10 days. That was it. When the house sold, he didn't give them one nickel. He put them on the street.

Dad wasn't always such a first-class asshole. His parents were good, decent, church-going folks. They taught right from wrong. Dad was good to everyone in the family until power and money fucked him up. He believed that because he had money he could treat everyone else like shit. And that he did. Except, of course, business associates and mobsters.

Ultimately, yes, I am responsible for the stupid-ass shit I did that got me in every kind of trouble imaginable, including three stints in the penitentiary. My antics put my parents through hell. But who knows? Had Dad at least been a decent human being, things may have turned out quite different. I know his brutality played a large role in my outright rebellion against him in every way.

One thing Dad liked to do was play golf. Dad loved to hang around white people, and the golf course is a mecca for the who's who in the Caucasian world. One spring day, just for the thrill of being an asshole, I found Dad's prized golf clubs in the garage. I took the knit covers off and poured globs of syrup on the woods, then pulled the covers back on. Knowing that he regularly played on Sundays, I did this on a Sunday evening so that Aunt Jemima would have a whole week to do her gloppy magic. The next Sunday, Dad followed his usual routine. He headed out into the garage to load the blue Titleist bag with his custom-fitted clubs into the trunk of the blue Caddy. Dad's color scheme always was blue, consistent with his Masonic lodge membership.

"Ah fuck!" the old man bellowed. "What the . . . shit, you little dumbass nigga." Dad charged into the house. He knew only I could have come up with this brilliant and devious plot. It didn't take long for him to get me and get me good. He cut off all my money for the summer. That meant no McDonald's, no movies, no new tennis shoes or sports cards.

Mom and Dad would often go off on weekend getaways, leaving Kevin and me with relatives. They knew better than to bring us along. One Fourth of July weekend I was exiled again to Aunt Bertha and Uncle Leroy's house in Cleveland Heights. Their kids, Ronnie and Linda, who were about six or seven years older than I, were shooting off fireworks on the sidewalk in front of the house along with some other friends. Naturally I wanted to go out and join in the mayhem, but one of Linda's friends held the door shut so I couldn't get out. I pushed and yelled and pushed some more, but no dice. Finally I yelled, "Fuck you, you bald-headed black bitch!" right there in front of Aunt Bertha.

"Chucky!" she yelled. "You can't talk to people like that."

"Like what?" I retorted.

"Don't call people those names."

"What names?"

"You know what you said."

"Whadaya talkin 'bout? I called her a bald-headed black fish." I was so clever.

Ronnie then came in. "We just don't want you to get hurt. It's for your own good." Interesting, because a few years later Ronnie helped me steal my mother's car. Where was the "for your own good" lecture then?

Like any other kids, we looked forward to Christmas every year. And like any other kids who had figured out the Santa thing, we searched the house every day from December 1st, looking for the stash of goods. One particular year, when I was about 10, we searched the house every day as usual but never found anything. We thought Mom and Dad had done an exceptional job of hiding the presents, so we got up on Christmas morning and headed downstairs. There was the tree, and beneath it was nothing. Nada.

"Where are the presents?" I pleaded with Mom. She just looked the other way.

"Oh well," Dad said very casually, and he flicked on the TV. I was traumatized. Just horrified. I cried all day long. Dad just watched golf. I cried all night long. Dad said nothing. The next morning, still nothing. I was still crying my ass off. Finally, he emerged from the bedroom with an armload of presents. I eventually calmed down, but even to this day this story just rips my heart out. Dad did what he did just because he could. It was his way of asserting control and getting back at me for being such a gallstone. If that meant traumatizing his children in the process, he didn't give a fuck.

Dad made it very clear that, to him, I wasn't worth a damn dollar. Many of the kids in the neighborhood attended St. Paschal's School in Highland Heights. My younger brother went to Benedictine High School, a private school in Cleveland. Dad didn't want to spend the money on me, so I went to public school. I'm sure that private school would have helped me stay on the rails, instead of associating with and fucking around with other kids like me who didn't give a shit.

Every Sunday, without fail, my brother and I were loaded into the Caddy and taken to Everlasting Missionary Baptist Church. Mom made us sing in the choir, and we absolutely hated it. Mom envisioned us as potential members of the Singing Angels (a top regional youth choir). What she got were two Chanting Gargoyles. During choir practice I would constantly pop my gum, which would constantly get me backhanded by the choir director, with the full knowledge and approval of my mommy dearest. We had to be there bright and early at 8 a.m. every Sunday, and the services would sometimes drag out to 2 p.m. That led to a lot of boredom, and when boredom sets in I go crazy.

One Sunday I decided to have a little fun. I snuck down into the choir room and bought a couple of Pepsis out of the vending machine. I shook up those cans and sprayed those bright emerald robes with streams of Pepsi. I sprayed every single robe. I was determined we weren't going to sing that day. When the choir came down for their robes, well, you imagine their reaction. And mine. But it wasn't my reaction that ratted me out. It was the fact that I was wearing my robe—the only one that was clean and dry. It didn't dawn on me that a clean robe would be, wait for it, a dead giveaway. My mission of musical espionage failed. We sang without our robes, and I got another bashing at my old man's hands when we got home.

It was at Everlasting that I met my good friend Tiny Man. Tiny Man and I have had many crazy experiences together over the years.

Reverend Smith was the pastor there at Everlasting. He was a good man, and he tried to be a father figure to me. But when he baptized me, he baptized the devil into my ass. I just didn't want to be there. When the offering plate came by, I would try to deftly snatch a 20-dollar bill or whatever I could get my grubby hands on. Rev. Smith tried to explain to me that I was an embarrassment to the family, and that I didn't realize just how good I had it. "People would love to be in your place," he would tell me. If you measured happiness by the shine of Cadillacs and custom grips on golf clubs, then he would have been right. But inside the four walls of our house, it was hell.

I wasn't original in the pranks I pulled. I would copy what I saw on TV—Daffy Duck, Tom and Jerry, and the way Popeye would always make an ass out of Bluto. At some fancy event at the Landerhaven party center, Mom and Dad both stepped away from the table for a few minutes, and Kevin and I, who didn't like the fact we were somewhere that we had to wear ties, decided to pull a prank we saw on the opening credits of an old episode of "Happy Days." We loosened the top of the saltshaker. Dad got back to the table, and soon thereafter that luscious golden caramelized porterhouse steak arrived. It sizzled and smelled divine clear across the room. Dad liked a little salt on his steak, but of course when he tried to shake a few grains out of the shaker, a small blizzard of salt dumped out.

"You little shit!" Dad yelled, knowing this was no accident, as he reached across the table and smacked me in the face. That was just the beginning. He finished it when we got home.

I always enjoyed causing a scene, especially if everyone eventually laughed. After gym class in the seventh grade, a couple of the guys bet me $10 to run around the gym naked. That was a no-brainer. As the next class lined up in the gym, I stripped down naked and bolted out. I ran around in circles, laughing away. The kids in the class, which was coed, were half in shock, half in hysterics. But I was doing what I do best—entertaining the crowd. After a few minutes of running around like a stark raving naked lunatic, I headed back to the locker room. The door was closed, so I gave it a tug. Damn! Those little shits who made the bet with me were on the other side holding the fuckin' door closed. I could hear those bastards on the other side of the door laughing away.

"Ramsey! Just what do you think you're doing?" the gym teacher demanded.

"Uh, I'm just trying to get in the locker room. Seems like this door is stuck."

"You idiot. Those guys pranked you. Get your clothes on and get to the office."

I did, and I was suspended.

CLASS DISMISSED

Education is not preparation for life; education is life itself.
—John Dewey

ONE OF MY BEST friends at Memorial Junior High was this Italian kid named Dominic. One day he gave me this nice wallet, just for the hell of it. That evening as I was watching TV, I took the wallet out and casually flipped it down on the coffee table. It was made of black leather, with the emblem of Laborers Local 860 stitched in gold. It caught Dad's attention.

"Where did you get that?" he asked, assuming, I'm sure, that I stole it.

"My Italian friend, Dominic, gave it to me," I said.

"Italian friend?" Dad asked. "What is his last name?"

"Liberatore."

"I see," Dad said. "What's his dad's first name?"

"I don't know," I said.

"Well, ask your friend at school tomorrow. Don't forget," Dad admonished me.

The next day I asked Dominic what was his dad's first name. He casually said, "Tony."

"Ok," I said, thinking nothing of it, and passed that on to Dad that evening.

The next day Dominic came home from school with me. Dad said to us, "Hey, guys, how would you like to go see 'Star Wars'? Then I'll drop you off back at your house, Dominic. Just show me where you live on our way to the theater." Of course we thought that would be a blast. When we turned onto Dominic's street, there in the driveway stood Dominic's father—Anthony Libera-tore. Yes, *the* Anthony Liberatore, the former business manager for the Laborers Local 860. The same guy who would later be tried and convicted of conspiracy in the car-bombing rubout of fellow mobster Danny Greene. Anthony Liberatore resembled actor Ray Liotta, who played a Mafioso role in "Goodfellas." Dad parked his Sedan de Ville and called out to him. Anthony's face lit up.

"Charlie!" he yelled with a smile that stretched all the way to Sicily. "It's been a long time!"

Dad jumped out of the car and they embraced. They obviously knew each other from some previous working relationship. Dad was a mid-level employee of the City of Cleveland. Yet he drove new Cadillacs, always had plenty of cash, played golf at the finest country clubs, and had a portfolio of hundreds of thousands of dollars of investments, which he never explained to my mother or anyone else. A connection to the mob? Nah, I'm sure he and Tony were just golfing buddies. Nothing to see here, folks. Move along.

They chatted for quite a while, to the point where Dominic and I thought we were in some sort of trouble. As those two carried on, Dominic and I decided to ditch the movie and head over to some girls' houses.

Dad's association with Anthony Liberatore presents a fair amount of questions.

Not long after we moved into Richmond Heights, our property was bombed. Twice. The first bomb took out the mailbox. The second bomb took out our porch. We were all scared, except Dad. He knew just what to do.

"I guess I better call some of my Italian friends and let them know what's going on," he said. So, Dad made a couple of calls. The next thing we knew, our mailbox was replaced and porch repaired.

As an eight grader at Memorial Junior High, with my good friend Liz Freeman.
(Liz Freeman Gregory)

"They said I should have told them it was me moving out here," Dad said.

Even more questions remain unanswered from the incident that put Dad permanently in a wheelchair. While in Florida on an alleged golfing trip in 2004, Dad had an "accident" that severed his spine. He claims he was just overcome by the heat and passed out or had a stroke, landing on his back across a golf cart. Yea, that kinda shit happens all the time.

*   *   *

Every summer Dad would line up some job for me. He was trying to keep me out of trouble, but of course I was too clever for that. One summer Dad got me a job in the Justice Center in downtown Cleveland. At first I thought this was going to be totally stupid and boring. Who wants to hang around with a bunch of stuffy lawyers and shit? When I got there the first day, I discovered that Dad had signed me up for a program for kids. That sounded a lot better, but there was one problem: These kids were all from the inner city, and being from suburban Richmond Heights, I didn't fit in. I might have been a pain-in-the-ass troublemaker, but these kids knew all about how to be professional criminals.

Anyway, this program had some of us working with the sheriff's office, some in the kitchen, some with the custodial staff. We became familiar with different parts of the building. Every day we would get together for lunch and talk about the different things we did. I, of course, was bored, which of course led to me thinking of something devious: a mass prison breakout! Just imagine how much fun it would be, I thought, to watch all those roaches scatter. Some of those guys deserved to be in jail; others really deserved to be in jail. What a hot nigga I would be if I could find a way to bust them all out.

Over the next few days, a bunch of us conspired over lunch. We knew that there was a central hub in the basement that had a main power switch. This hub was locked in a cage with a padlock. If we could bust open that hub, I could get in there and throw the main switch off. Since the cell doors in the jail were electronically controlled, I figured that if I could cut the power to the whole building, the doors wouldn't stay locked and the convicts could run free. There wasn't anyone in particular who I wanted to free, and I wasn't on some prison mercy project or some other ACLU silly-ass shit. I just wanted to see those fuckers all run amok and tell me how cool I was. It would be hilarious.

I had the kids who worked with the custodial staff find a hammer. A few others were lookouts, and few others just wanted to watch the master in action. We made it to the basement of the Justice Center and down to the power hub. Of course there was a lot of giggling and carrying on, which got the attention of a janitor who was hiding down there to smoke a cigarette. He overheard us and called in on his radio that something was going down in the basement. I took that hammer and, with three well-aimed whacks, bashed open the fucking lock. I entered the cage and saw high overhead the main switch lever. It was a big lever, not just a button. It was time for my Michael Jordan moment. Whenever Michael Jordan had his tongue flapping out it meant he was about to do something awesome. I stuck my tongue out, just like Mike, because I was about to do something even more fucking awesome. I reached for that lever, readied my leap and . . .

"FREEZE, YOU MOTHERFUCKER!"

It was just like the scene out of "The Blues Brothers" movie, when Dan Aykroyd and John Belushi finally pay the tax bill for the orphanage and turn around to see a whole battalion of soldiers pointing rifles at them. In this case, it was a battalion of Cuyahoga County sheriffs all pointing their guns at me. Ah, shit. My great idea had been foiled by that fuckin' janitor.

"Ah, eh, I'm just tryin' to help all the prisoners," I pleaded.

They took me to an office, where one of the program directors said, "Fuck, it's that Ramsey kid. Better call his dad."

Dad came and took me home. "Just how the hell do you manage to get yourself into all this shit?" he asked. "How the fuck do you come up with these damn ideas all on your own?"

Life between Dad and me was a constant chess match. I would be the white pieces, Dad was the black. In chess, the white player leads the attack. The black player sets up a strategic defense. Dad tried to anticipate my moves, finding ways to cut me off at the pass. I always found ways to work around his defenses. Dad was a very smart, self-educated, mean bastard. I was just as smart, but not mean—I just didn't give a shit about you. Since Dad held all the money, he also held the ultimate checkmate, but I never let that stop me from doing crazy shit.

Then there was the time around 1985 when Dad was hosting a party, a real who's who in Richmond Heights gathering. The mayor, city council, policemen, anyone who was anyone was there. Dad was standing in the living room when it sounded like a rock hit the window. But it was no rock. It was a bullet. But it didn't penetrate, because Dad had the windows replaced with bulletproof glass. Obviously he was thinking ahead.

Then there was the time that Dad won some sort of special key that opened a door to a private dinner club at the Cleveland Play House. We were invited to see a performance of "The Nutcracker," something I thought would be as exciting as a flat tire. Mom told Kevin and me that there was to be no after-school snack, and that we would dress up nice and meet Dad at the Play House for dinner and the show. I was determined that, yes, indeed, it was going to be quite a show.

While at school all day, I drank as much water as I could. I held my piss all day, so much I could practically taste it. Talk about learning discipline. When we got home, I got dressed, still determined to hold the dam back. I was wigglin' and jumpin' everywhere, and finally I decided I had to let some of it out. So I let maybe 40 percent out, but kept on drinking.

"Why are you drinking all that water?" Mom asked.

"Uh, I played a lot of basketball at school today with Ronnie and the guys. Got really dehydrated." There was no Ronnie; I just made all that up, like I did whenever the situation made it convenient. We headed for the Play House, and I kept jumping around.

"Stop that, Chucky. You look like you're going to piss your pants." I thought maybe Mom was on to me, but I just kept on drinking. We met up with Dad at the restaurant. All I wanted was water. And more water. Finally, we got to the theater. We were escorted to our seats by formally clad ushers wearing white gloves and red velvet vests. Oh yes, this was going to be a festive evening.

Mom got to show off one of her finest furs, and she was so proud that she was teaching her sons about fine culture. Heh heh, bitch, I was about to teach everyone about piss.

The lights went down, and so did my pants. I jumped up and just let it fly. I pissed all over Kevin. All over Mom. All over Dad. All over the people in front of us.

"You muddafuck . . ." Dad said with great restraint as he tackled me, pulled my pants up, and dragged me off to the men's room. What a show I put on for all those very nice white people.

Another one of my favorite stunts was the time I got back at Mom for not letting me hang with some kids from Mayfield Heights, a neighboring suburb. It was populated with Italians, Jews, and Germans, and I was friendly with them all, but for some reason my mother thought that the kids from Mayfield were just trouble. So when Mom told me I wasn't allowed to go golfing with some Mayfield kids, I decided to once again even the score.

Mom enjoyed the lavish lifestyle of the wealthy suburban wife. She loved her furs and jewelry and, of course, didn't care where money came from as long as it just kept coming. And of course she loved to go shopping. So one day, before Mom went out on one of her shopping excursions, I thought I'd prepare a little surprise for her. No, I wasn't going to take the money out of her purse. I'd already done that so many times that it was too boring. This time, I got a couple packs of Wrigley's gum and just chewed away until I got all the flavor out of them. I wadded up a huge gumball, then pulled it apart piece by piece and stuck it on all the cash in Mom's purse. Not just a few gum chunks here and there. I patiently stuck all those bills together with hundreds of little gum wads. Then I put the stack of the bills on the floor and jumped up and down on it to make sure the gum was squished around real good. All in all, I probably fucked up about $500 in cash. When Mom came home she proceeded to beat the black off of me.

In my teenage years I probably had 15 or so near-death experiences at the hands of my parents.

"I wish you'd leave and never come back," Mom once said. So, I took her up on it. I headed over to the game room at Richmond Mall. Somehow she found me, and she took me home to yet another of those near-death experiences.

Another time she just blurted out, "What the fuck is wrong with you? Why do you do the things you do? Sometimes I feel I failed you."

"I think you're right," I said. SMACK!

There was another time when I freaked out the white folk. One of Dad's favorite aunts died in Florida, so we made the trip for the funeral. Dad was taking care of all the arrangements, so on the day of the funeral we got there early. While Mom and Dad were occupied with the last-minute details and arriving friends and family, I decided to look around to see if I could create a horror movie, at least in my mind. Any door that wasn't locked, I opened. I saw mostly storage closets and offices, nothing too scary, but I did wander into another parlor where there were two coffins. One was open and had a dead guy in it. The other was closed, so, of course, I had to open it. I lifted the lid and saw that it was empty. This, of course, was an open invitation for me to get in it. So I climbed in, closed the lid, and giggled as I munched on some Scooby Snacks I had stashed in my suit coat pocket.

Meanwhile, the funeral service in the other parlor for my aunt was starting, and I was nowhere to be found. My mother began looking all around for me, but I remained hidden in the coffin, perfectly content to wait it out. The funeral service was going to be boring. In this coffin I could pretend to be a zombie or something while munching away. That would be much more fun. Then I heard some voices in the parlor. I didn't recognize them—these were voices of white folks. They had come in to view the poor stiff in the other, open coffin. I heard one of them say, "Why is this other coffin in this room?" Someone else said they would ask the funeral director.

That was my cue. I popped out like a jack-in-the-box, my suit all wrinkled, tie all sideways, crumbs smeared on my smiling face.

"Ta-da!" I announced. "Hello everybody!"

Those poor white folks let out a terrifying shriek. My, oh my, I had no idea Caucasians could be so damn emotional! Old ladies were screaming. Kids were crying. Even the funeral director let out a yell. I just smiled, did a little twirl, and jumped down to the floor. These trembling white folks looked like they just saw their first black ghost. Now this was how a funeral should be. Fun times for all, and I was the star of the show!

Mom heard the commotion from the other side of the funeral home and quickly concluded only one person could possibly be responsible. The funeral director grasped my wrist and led me out into the hallway, meeting my mother halfway.

"Is this your son?" he asked angrily.

"Dammit. Just what did he do now?"

"He just jumped out of a coffin at the service in the other parlor. Poor people are freaked out."

Mom grabbed me by the arm, took me into a side room, and whaled the batfuck outta me.

*   *   *

I'm sure the staff at Memorial Junior High popped champagne corks the day I left. Because I repeated the seventh grade, they had to put up with me an extra year. It was off to Brush High School, where I would manage to get myself expelled in just a year.

My partner in crime was this Russian Jew kid, Leonid. We screwed around together and found ways to cause all sorts of shit. In the boys' locker room, the guys would put their regular clothes in lockers that weren't locked. So Leonid and I would sneak in there during gym class—not to steal, but to fuck things up. We did shit like take their clothes and soak them in the shower, then put them back. Some of the guys would keep a water bottle in their lockers, and I thought it would be hysterical to piss in a few of them. That didn't work very well, as the guys were able to smell it before taking a swig. So next time, Leonid came up with a more devious plan.

"Here," he said. "Put this in your mouth." It looked like an ordinary piece of some sort of vegetable. I popped it my mouth.

"SHIT!" I roared, with dragon-like flames spewing from my eyes and mouth. "Goddammit! That shit is hot!" I found the nearest water fountain and nearly drained Lake Erie. I had experienced nothing like that in my life. "What the fuck was that?" I asked between burning gasps. Talk about *muy caliente!*

"Habanero," Leonid said while laughing with snot shooting out of his nose. Habanero is one of the hottest peppers in the world. He then proceeded to rub the juices of that muthafucka of fire on the rims and lids of all the water bottles he could find. He went into the gym teacher's office and rubbed it on whistles, toothbrushes, and coffee mugs. We then hid out. The guys came back from gym class, and the fun began. We were mere freshman, and these were upperclassmen. These guys were gagging and screaming, running around like the Germans were attacking with mustard gas. Leonid and I couldn't help ourselves. We doubled over in laughter, and continued laughing our asses off as those upperclassmen found us and proceeded to whale the fuck out of us. The more they pounded on us, the more we laughed. We got beat up pretty bad, but it was oh so worth it.

I can't begin to remember how many times I got my ass beat by a paddle. I got paddled almost every day. Again, it wasn't because I was trying to be mean; I was just trying to be funny. But the teachers and administrators just didn't get my humor. Boys were paddled regularly at Memorial, girls hardly ever. Some teachers would whack you right there in front of the class; others would take you out in the hall, make you drop your pants, and whack you there. I remember one teacher constantly whacking my ass. He had a paddle that had holes in it in order to reduce wind resistance. Constantly the morning announcements would end with, ". . . and Chuck Ramsey, report to the office." If the bell would ring and I was still in the hallway, I was routinely sent to the office.

*　　*　　*

There was a time my brother and I were just bored. There were two cars in the driveway—Dad's Sedan de Ville and his city-owned car. Dad always owned a Sedan de Ville. He wasn't single, so an El Dorado wouldn't work, and since he wasn't a pimp he didn't get a Fleetwood.

"Wanna go somewhere?" I asked Kevin.

"Sure," he said. We had no specific place to go, but the fun of getting there was too much to resist. We found the keys to Dad's city car, jumped in, and headed off. We drove around Beachwood and Richmond Heights, finally deciding to head over to our friend Nicolas' house in Shaker Heights. While we were there just watching TV, Nick's dad came up to us.

"Uh, Chucky, does your dad know you're driving around in his city car?"

"Uh, no."

"Well, he's about to."

When we got home, Dad made us walk from Richmond Heights to Shaker Heights—about six miles—to apologize to Nick's parents. He made sure we had no money so we couldn't hop a bus. When we got home, Mom half killed me. To even the score, I found a box of her wigs, took them out to the back yard, and set them on fire.

Yes, I was an asshole. But I was not a bully. I didn't seek or get into any major confrontations. Practical jokes and making people laugh were my specialties. I would follow teachers down the hall, mimicking their every step. I enjoyed the novelty of being the sole chocolate chip in the mix.

I didn't cut every class. A few I sometimes found interesting. For example, I liked Home Ec. Two reasons: It was filled with pretty girls, and I got to eat what I cooked. I also sometimes enjoyed math. I liked the teacher, Mr. Love. He was a Mason, as was my dad. Dad was a 33rd degree Mason, the highest rank possible. Because of that connection, Mr. Love watched out for me a bit. If I needed a hall pass for whatever reason, he'd help me out. Mr. Love found it interesting how I did my math problems. For me, it made a whole lot more sense when I put dollar signs in front of the numbers.

School meant nothing to me other than an outlet to mess around and meet girls. If they were Jewish, I'd tell them I was Jewish. And the girls didn't have to be students. There was one teacher I thought was rather hot, so I stole one of Dad's credit cards and tried to give it to her to impress her.

Sometimes I would help kids who got picked on. I remember coming to the aid of Mike Trivisonno Jr., son of the popular Cleveland radio talk show host Mike Trivisonno Sr. Mike Jr. was a short kid, but I stood up for him. If I saw any racist shit going on, I didn't personally jump in the fray but would convince some white kid to go pound the racist white kid. I'd convince some Jewish kid to take care of it. That way my hands stayed clean while the racist kid would get popped by a crazy Israeli, as I would say.

*   *   *

I had long ago decided what I wanted to do for a living. It was simple. I wanted to be a billionaire. Just how was I going to become a billionaire? That was simple, too. I remember watching some blond surfer dude appear on "The Dinah Shore Show." He invented something by accident and was now this multi-zillionaire, and yet he didn't even have a high school education. Now that's the career path I wanted to follow. Just think of something brilliant and collect millions. Dad had all this money, and he didn't seem to work very hard. Why not me?

Mom quickly changed the channel. "Don't you pay no mind to what that stupid white man just said," she said. "You need to get your education like a proper Christian boy should."

Just plain bored with school, one day I decided to head over to Scotto Pizza at Richmond Mall. I had an older friend, Pete, who had a car. I asked him if I could use his car for a while, and being the pretty cool dude he was, he tossed me the keys. I drove his cranberry-colored 1978 Buick Regal to the mall and got myself some pizza. On the way back, since I was in no hurry to get back to school, I thought I'd take a cruise around the neighboring suburbs of South Euclid, Richmond Heights, and Lyndhurst. Sure enough, as I was cruising down Belvoir Boulevard, radio blasting away, a police car pulled up behind me. He followed me for a few miles then flicked on his lights. OK, I figured, time to play Starsky and Hutch. I floored it. Not knowing where to go, for some reason I thought I should head back to Brush High School. Zipping along Glenlyn Road to where it curved left into Daytona Road (a most appropriate name considering the speed I was haulin'), I thought I could lose the cop amid the cars in the parking lot. I was going to drive through the lot and out the back exit. I drove through the lot, thinking for sure I shook him. But there at the back exit, waiting for me, was another cop car. Trapped!

The cops grabbed me and took me not to the police station but to the principal's office, where my parents were called. Dad showed up, Mom didn't. I wasn't charged with any crime. The authorities all knew Dad rather well and left it up to him to decide what to do with me. He hauled my ass home and dished out his justice the way he knew how.

That was one suspension too many. The decision was made to expel me. That didn't bother me at all, as I was looking forward to more fuckaround time.

"There's still hope for your sorry ass yet," Dad said. "You are going to get a GED and then continue to college." I was only 15, and as much as I wanted to assert my independence, Dad wasn't about to grant it to me. I had no alternative. Disobeying Dad's orders was just another way of asking to be a punching bag.

The GED class was held at Cleveland Heights High School, from 5 to 10 p.m. Monday through Friday, for a month. Each week we were to take on a different subject. Most of the students were in their 30s through their 50s. At 15, I was the youngest one there. And the cleverest. Mom would drop me off at the school just before 5 p.m.

"I'm so proud of you, Chucky," she would say.

Yeah, right, thanks for the lift, you dumb bitch, I thought to myself. Instead of going to the class, I took a 5:45 bus to Severance Center and headed to the bowling alley and pool hall. There, I would trim one sucka for $200 playing 9 ball, another sucka for $100 playing 8 ball. I would then catch the 8:45 bus back to the school and poke my head in the class for a few minutes, always having some creative excuse for my nearly four-hour tardiness. Mom would pick me up at 10, none the wiser. Since this wasn't real school, I wasn't really truant, and no one called my parents to rat me out.

I continued this pattern almost every day, until one day while at the pool hall I fired home the winning 8 ball shot in a side pocket, turned around to accept the congrats from the boys, and saw Dad standing there, arms folded, face scowling. Someone had tipped him off.

"Is this some kind of field trip, you dumb nigga?"

Punishment was, as usual, swift and severe. I learned my lesson for a few days. I kept Dad convinced that I was sitting through class, while all along I kept heading back to the pool hall whenever I could.

Finally, the day of the final exam arrived. I took the test, not sure of how well I did. A week or so later, a large brown envelope arrived in the mail. I opened it carefully. There in my hands was my GED certificate. I had passed that damn test with an 88 fuckin' percent! I was no dumb nigga. I was smooth and smart—smarter than everyone else. I could spend three quarters of my time hustlin' at the pool hall and still pass that fuckin' test. The real idiots, it was clear to me, were those dumbshits who were wasting their time at that dumbass high school.

My parents were in a state of disbelief. Real disbelief. Mom burned up the phone line to Columbus, calling around to find out just how I pulled off this latest shenanigan.

"There's no way in hell this little fucker could have passed that test," Mom kept yelling into the phone at whatever unfortunate soul would take the call. "He couldn't even handle the seventh grade. This is obviously a sick joke, or whoever graded that test doesn't know what the hell they're doing." But every time she called, she kept getting the same answer: My score was legit. Eventually Mom took that certificate and had it laminated.

HIGHER EDUCATION

A man who has never gone to school may steal from a freight car; but if he has a university education, he may steal the whole railroad.

—Theodore Roosevelt

FIFTEEN YEARS OLD, AND done with high school. I had convinced myself that the world had been outsmarted by this nigga. Dad, though, was still in charge of me, which I didn't like, but there wasn't much I could do about that. Still in disbelief that I had passed the GED with flying colors, Dad said that it didn't stop here. Now that I had this GED certification, I needed to do something with it other than admire a laminated piece of paper on the wall.

Dad's favorite cousin was the president of Knoxville College in Tennessee, a small, historically black college. Dad wasn't sure that I'd learn anything, but he thought that at least I'd be monitored. I liked the idea of getting out of the house and out of his abusive control.

The day came that we loaded up the Sedan de Ville for the nine-hour drive down Interstates 71 and 75. Mom cried as we left, not because this was a big day in her baby's life, but because she knew I'd be back.

I turned 16 just as school was starting in the fall of 1985. I was independent and could pretty much do what I wanted to do. School? What was that? I had a roommate, some guy from Indianapolis we called Ali. He had gotten to college the more traditional way of hard work and study through four years of high school. He envied the fact that I beat the system and was there at 16. Because Dad had given me a wad of cash and would wire me what I needed for school, I quickly became the most popular guy in the dorm. I was too young to buy beer, but I funded the supply for the entire dorm with Dad's money. Anybody needed money, I would help him out. This kept even the toughest and biggest muthafuckas at my disposal.

Not only had I beat the system, I was going to live life to the fullest.

It took me maybe 72 hours to get into trouble.

Just outside the campus were the projects, the slummy part of Knoxville. Guys in the projects looked at the college guys as rich and snobbish. My newly formed posse and I decided we needed to get some beer. Not just any beer, but Olde English 800. If you wanted beer for social purposes, you bought Miller. But if you wanted beer so you could become ignorant, Olde English 800, or "8-ball," was the ticket. It was a smooth and sweet malt liquor, packing more of a punch than Colt 45. So we walked the half-mile to the convenience store to get some. After we paid for the beer with Dad's money, a group of the local project slugs stopped us at the door.

"How much money you got there, niggaboy?" one of them asked menacingly.

"Uh . . ." I fumbled through my pocket. "I got seven dollars."

"Good enough for today," he said as he snatched it out of my hand. From that point on, I realized that these guys controlled the streets. Every time I walked into a store or any establishment in their hood, I would have to either buy my way out or fight my way out. For me, the first option was more practical. I always made sure I had a few extra bucks to buy myself out of any situation.

I never attended a single class. In fact, I never even registered for a single class. I was enjoying the college experience too much. Parties, girls, road trips, girls, beer, girls. It just didn't stop.

I would call Dad and make up some story about how I needed to get this super-expensive textbook for this class, and ask him to wire me $500. No problem. We needed money for a road trip to Florida. I called Dad, told him there was an expensive lab fee due. Another thousand dollars, no problem. Dad wasn't stupid. I'm sure he knew I was up to no good, but this was keeping me out of his house. If one of the female students needed a little help with tuition money, well, I was the man. I could make it happen, in exchange for certain personal services.

I kept beating a path to the Western Union office, and by the end of the semester I had easily fucked away $20,000 of Dad's money. This was the life! Do whatever I wanted to do, go wherever I wanted to go, endless supply of women, and Dad just unknowingly kept greasing the rails with his cash.

During Christmas break, my report card arrived at home. Dad insisted on seeing it. He sat down and looked at it, then looked at me. He looked at it again, then looked at me again. I knew trouble was brewing, that he knew I had been scamming him.

"This says you have a grade point average of 0.00. Just what the fuck are you doing there, you stupidass muthafuckin' nigga? You even got an F in LUNCH! How did you manage to get a fuckin' F in fuckin' lunch?"

Hmm. Well, I guess there were too many times when they used square bread instead of circular. Threw me off. Then there was the time when we were supposed to bring saltine crackers and I brought Ritz. Lunch can be very hard.

Still, Dad was determined to do whatever he could to keep me out of the house. Despite my racking up that 0.00 GPA and blowing a huge chunk of his money, he took me back to Knoxville College for the second semester. This time, though, he gave me not a dime.

I started college at age 16, racking up a perfect grade point average of 0.00 at Knoxville College. *(Charles Ramsey collection.)*

With the flow of easy cash cut off, I now had no reason to accomplish anything.

The last straw came shortly after I returned. Just before the end of the previous semester I had tried out for the basketball team. The head coach was a good ol' Southern boy, and good ol' Southern boys were the type he wanted on the team. I wasn't one of them. I was cut. I'm sure my 0.00 GPA would have come into play sooner or later as to my eligibility, but I wasn't thinking that far ahead. I was just pissed as hell that I, the smartest and most popular nigga in America, or at least at Knoxville College, wasn't just automatically put on the team. So I decided that one day while they were playing on the road I would get a little revenge. I made my way to the storage area of the gym, and after a few Olde Englishes, I took a knife and sliced up every basketball I could find. I then proceeded back to my dorm, which also housed six of the players on the team. Locked doors meant nothing to me other than a slight inconvenience, so I climbed out on a window ledge and pushed my way in through windows. I trashed the shit out of those rooms, took some clothes I wanted, spread shaving cream all over the place, pissed wherever I felt like. That took a lot of energy, and so after fuckin' up the sixth room, I was tired. Since the team was on the road, I just lay down in the bed and went to sleep like this was the Holiday Inn.

About 2 a.m., I felt this fist smash into my face. Holy shit! These guys came back early! I staggered up, only to get punched in the gut by some big guy. I don't know how many guys were in the room, but they were gangbanging me a good one. I was too bleary-eyed to see anything, and all I could hear was "you goddamn nigga" and the sound of fists pounding my face. Lucky for me a security guard showed up and helped me fight my way out of the room.

I was taken to the security center, where they called Dad. That afternoon Dad arrived, and instead of driving back to Cleveland he continued on to Birmingham, to my grandparents' house. Ordinarily, Dad might have beat the shit out of me as well, but instead he got a kick out of the fact that those guys did the heavy lifting for him.

"Heh, heh, look at you. You look like a nigga raccoon," Dad laughed, noticing that's how a black guy with two black eyes looks. "I'd knock the black out of you myself, but those boys saved me the trouble."

I was quickly and quietly expelled from Knoxville College, yet faced no criminal charges.

You would think that this would spell the end of my attempt at a college education, but Dad wasn't ready to give up. The last thing he wanted was for me to wind up back at home. After three days of golf in Alabama, he drove me back up north but made a detour to Wilberforce, Ohio, to the campus of Central State University. Central State is another historically black college, located between Cincinnati and Columbus, with an enrollment of about 2,000 students. Dad went straight to the dean's office and hauled me in with him.

"Sit your ass down there," Dad said, pointing to a chair off to the side. It was clear that Dad had been on the phone with the dean and that he had already made the necessary arrangements.

"Well, here he is," Dad said. "Ya think you can do anything with him?"

"Hmm, I'm not Jesus," the dean said, "but I'll do what I can." He then handed me a key to my dorm room.

I had a roommate, Maurice, who graduated from John Adams High School in Cleveland. Maurice was from the streets, yet he was as cool as fuck. We were two very opposite individuals. He knew where he'd come from, the mean streets of Cleveland, and he knew the consequences that failure would bring. Maurice didn't want a life hustlin' on the East Side streets; he was focused and made sure he did the right thing. As for me, I just didn't give a shit. The old man always paid for everything, and if I bombed out of school he'd still pay for everything. I never feared having to wallow in my own shit. I was still a minor. Dad couldn't just lock me out of the house.

At first I actually attended some classes. Not because I had a sudden surge of ambition, but because there were about 25 women in every class. I even caught part of a seminar that featured Don King, Mike Tyson, and Bill Cosby. Cosby was the only one who made some sort of sense, saying that if the future of black America was saggy pants, then we were in deep shit, or words to that effect.

The flow of cash from Dad continued. I engaged in the same pattern as before. I looked for women who needed a little help meeting their expenses, and you can figure it out from there. I blew through another $10,000 or so of Dad's money but still wanted a little more excitement. So I took up a hobby—cooking crack cocaine. I learned how to mix the powder cocaine with the right amount of baking soda and water, then cook it just the right amount of time, reducing the heat at the precise moment. Then freeze it for five minutes. This turned the final product into just the right density so that it could be easily broken up into $20 rocks. I thought I was hot shit when I hung around drug dealers because I could relate to them. They were rich and ruthless, and so was I. We just got our money from different sources. I'd knock the fuck out of you and take your $40, only to spend it on your girlfriend so I could bang her, and then she could get back to you and complain how you don't have any money.

I got myself hooked up with this dude "Lucky" who showed me the ropes. Rocks were for smokers, powder was for snorters, so it was good to have both in your inventory. Lucky took me to a spot on the slummier side of Dayton and told me to just stay put. He then walked down the street and told the people hanging around that I had the good shit. One by one, they came up to me and handed me twenty-dollar bills. I was amazed. The cocaine sold itself. I didn't have to do much else other than stand there and fill the orders. It didn't take long before I had run out of merchandise and had hundreds of dollars in my pocket. Pretty soon I had built up a steady, reliable clientele. I had no problem making $250 or so tax-free cash every day. Yes, I saw a lot of fights and a lot of shootings, but I was crafty enough to stay away from that. I was strictly business—I saw many addicts yack their guts out on the streets, begging for anything, but if they didn't have $20 they got nothing from me. I was a pretty big dude and had strong street cred, so I didn't have to carry a gun. I wasn't interested in robbing or fucking someone up, I just wanted to make assloads of cash.

Dayton was the perfect place to sell crack. It was situated along a central pipeline that came from the south and then diverted either toward Chicago or Detroit. The suppliers were true professionals—they knew how not to get caught, and they made sure they never had physical possession of the shit for more than 24 hours. It was fast, easy money, and within a few months I had accumulated about $30,000 in cash, which I kept stashed in my '82 Buick Skylark, which I bought with cash. Since you need a driver's license to register a car and I had none, I just had a woman from Central State register it in her name.

I went to parties at the University of Cincinnati, Wright State, Ohio State, University of Akron, Kent State, as many and as often as I could. I never sold drugs to college kids; I was just looking for an easy fuck. I also didn't party with crackheads. I never feared running out of customers; I only feared running out of drugs.

Having all that easy cash posed a problem. I couldn't exactly deposit it at the local bank, and I couldn't bring it home with me. I had no choice but to blow it. I blew thousands at strip clubs in Dayton and Cincinnati, and on nice clothes and meals at fine restaurants. I paid for tuition and books for many young women.

With women I always used a condom. It wasn't that I was exercising some semblance of good judgment; I was just too selfish to see myself ever giving a fuck what happens after I had my time with you. Children would mean accountability, and I wasn't about to have any of that shit. I didn't want to know your last name, and after the second orgasm I was done with your ass.

Needless to say, I wasn't exactly setting any academic records at Central State. My old man didn't check up on me. We never communicated other than when he came down to haul my ass away. He just wanted me to stay the hell away from Northeast Ohio. As long as I wasn't coming home, he didn't give a fuck what I did. When we did talk, he always told me that Cleveland wasn't big enough for both of us. I talked to Mom every couple of weeks and kept her thinking I was giving an effort at school.

One night, just for shits and giggles, I decided to break into Banneker Hall, the science building, and steal some computers. I had no idea what I would do with them, but the thrill of the hunt was too enticing. I found an open window and pulled my lanky body through. I found the computer room and stacked up about a half-dozen computers by the door, then began looking through some desks for whatever interesting items I might find. Little did I know that I had tripped a silent alarm. As I was riffling through a desk, someone flicked on the light.

"Can I help you?" this hulking security guard asked.

I just stood there. I knew I had been caught. This guy was about twice my size, so getting past him and through the door just wasn't going to happen.

"Oh, it's you," he said. I didn't recognize this guy but apparently he had been told about me. "What a fucking embarrassment you are to your old man." When anyone told me I was a fuckup and mentioned the old man, they had my attention. I didn't care what Dad thought of me, but I did care that the endless supply of money continued.

I was escorted to the campus security office. "Well, do you want to call him or should I?" the security officer asked. I sure didn't want to. So yet again, Dad got that all-too-familiar phone call. While the officer spoke to him, I could hear Dad on the other end. It was short and to the point.

"Mr. Ramsey," the officer said. "This is the Central State security office."

"Goddammit. What the fuck did that nigga do now?"

By 7 a.m., Dad was there at the security office, once again hauling my ass back to the car. "Now what? Just what in hell am I going to do with you now? I knew you were going to get your Ph.D. degree. I knew it. You finally got that Ph.D., muthafucka."

"Ph.D.? Whaddaya talkin' 'bout?" I asked.

"Post-hole digger. That's all you've got the brains for, you dumb-shit. You'll never be more than a goddamn post-hole digger. You'll always be Chucky, the post-hole digger nigger."

Dad had finally caught on that college was not my thing. Well, it was my thing only as long as I could keep the circle of money, drugs, cars and women in motion.

When we got back to Richmond Heights, Dad figured out my next move. He didn't consult with me; he just told me. I had no say. That's the kind of control he had. I knew better than to protest or put up a fight. No black dude ever got into a fight with his dad and lived to tell about it.

"I know what you can do," he said. "Asbestos removal."

Dad registered me in an asbestos-removal certification class at the University of Cincinnati. The problem was, as usual, that this would involve attending classes, something that clearly didn't sit well with me. Luckily, attendance was never taken in any of the classes, and I maybe got in a grand total of 45 minutes of class time over the four-week program. All I had to do to get my certification was to pass the test at the end. There was an important chart in the text from the Occupational Safety and Health Administration (OSHA), and I memorized it. I then took the test and, just like with my GED, I aced it. I was now a certified asbestos remover. Lucky me.

While attending the certification program, I met a friend whose parents had an asbestos-removal business in Jacksonville, Florida. He asked me to come down there and work in the family business. The idea of leaving the icy Ohio winters, as well as my parents, behind had a very strong appeal, so I packed up and moved to Jacksonville. I had just turned 18, and although I had been living like an independent adult for a few years, now it was finally legal. When I got to Jacksonville, I stayed at one cheap hotel after another. I was paid $13 an hour, cash under the table, and the company paid the rent. That was pretty good money, and of course I had no sense of budgeting or prioritizing. I took a taxi everywhere I had to go. I'd spend $12 on a cab ride to get a $5 meal at McDonald's. I spent my money like a drunken congressman spends yours: prime rib, steaks, shrimp, lobster, knock-off Rolexes and Gucci, marijuana, and any slag whore who would take $40.

But I just didn't fit in with the South. Southern boys wanted to do business with Southern boys. My Cadillac-and-champagne lifestyle didn't help, either. I decided to pack it all up and come back to Cleveland.

Dad decided that he would put me to work for his company, General Communications Inc. As a minority-owned business, and with his many insider contacts, Dad easily got a half-million dollar contract to remove asbestos in the Cleveland Public Schools.

"Heh, heh, with all this minority set-aside shit, I'm sure glad I'm a nigga, oh Lord, otherwise I wouldn't get shit," Dad would chuckle.

I was assigned to the crew, and of course the free room and board were sufficient pay in his mind. To Dad, money was his only concern. Dad would never express any emotion over what happened to a human being, but if his money was involved he would go ballistic. So, just because I felt like it, I came up with a genius plan of evil fuckery.

OSHA would install monitors in asbestos removal worksites for obvious reasons. As long as the monitors showed the levels were acceptable, you could work a normal shift. Wear a rubbery-smelling respirator, change your protective clothing, and you're fine. If the monitors showed too high a reading, an OSHA team would have to be called in. And if the readings were high enough, OSHA had the ability to scrap your program. So my goal was to cause those monitors to register so high that the project would have to be scrapped, and Dad would be out a couple hundred thousand of the taxpayers' dollars. There was nothing in it for me other than the satisfaction of fucking things up for the old man.

The first thing you must do when removing asbestos is to saturate the hell out of it. We would use these pressure bottles with wands, similar to those you get at the hardware store filled with weed killer. Then we'd soak that shit until it turns into mud. That would prevent dust from forming during the removal process, and dust is what gets into your lungs and fucks you up.

We were working on a school building that sat on the site now occupied by the Cleveland State University Wolstein Center. After everyone went home for the day, I stayed behind. Because Dad was the boss, I normally stayed late every day to lock up. So no one suspected anything. I put on my astronaut suit, donned a mask and respirator, and climbed up the scaffolding. I found all sorts of asbestos-covered pipes that no one had soaked. I took my cutting knife and sliced the shit out of everything I could reach. The asbestos opened up like a baked potato and rained down what looked like bags of flour. I created such an asbestos cloud that I couldn't see three feet in front of me. I then climbed down the goddamn scaffolding, took my protective suit off, showered in the containment room, and headed home.

The next morning, I took a long detour to work. I stopped by McDonald's and got Sausage McMuffins and coffee for the crew. When I arrived at the job site, everyone, including Dad, was just standing around.

"What's the problem?" I asked so innocently, acting like I didn't hear all the alarms blaring away.

"Fuck!" Dad yelled, looking at me. "I'm sure you had nuthin' to do with this, you no-good goddamn nigga."

I just looked away and handed out hash browns and coffee to the newly unemployed saps. OSHA came to investigate, determined that the site was too contaminated, and the project was canceled. I had just cost him a couple hundred thousand dollars. Checkmate, asshole.

With the project now cancelled, Dad got me a job at Eli Wrecking, where I could do something I did well: destroy things. But that wasn't the end to my fucking up the old man's business. Dad's bank account usually had a few hundred thousand dollar balance. How did I know? Glad you asked. Remember, Dad's name is Charles Ramsey, with no middle name, and my name is also Charles Ramsey, no middle name. So I had no problem walking into the Huntington Bank in Richmond Heights and withdrawing thousands of dollars in cash whenever I damn well pleased. I figured he was just too much of a dumbfuck to notice the difference, and besides, there was plenty more where that came from. I bought myself not just a pair of Air Jordans, but every pair of Air Jordans I could find in the fucking store. I also bought every Air Jordan sweat suit I could find, and plenty for my friends, too. In a period of about six weeks, I casually helped myself to about $50,000 in Dad's account.

I ate, along with my friends, at all the nice restaurants, bought four Guess watches with interchangeable bands, and all the Izod, Nautica and Ralph Lauren shit I could put on my black ass. I toted around town in my shiny black 1986 Chevy Blazer, paid for of course by my old man as a Christmas gift, before I had helped myself to his cash. But what good was a Chevy Blazer without a hot chick riding around with me? I knew I had to pimp it out. But I knew better than to put on custom wheels or do much of anything to the exterior because that would draw the attention of the old man. The best way to get the most female attention without Dad noticing anything would be to put in a kickass Kicker box. I took my Blazer to Five Star Music and Audio on Libby Road in Maple Heights. "Give me something that will be so goddamn loud that babies will cry. White people will call the police and even Jesus himself to tell me to turn it down. I want to be heard in Akron while I drive down Euclid Avenue in Cleveland. Can you make that happen, Swami?" I asked the shop owner.

"Ah, yessir, we make it loud," he said. And he wasn't kidding. Shit!

The first thing he did was put in a 500-watt Kicker box. That was just for starters. He replaced the factor 5-watt radio with a two-channel 50-watt radio and cassette deck, with a 400-watt amp hooked up to that. All in all, I had a thousand fucking watts blasting though that sound system. I would blast "Jump" by Kriss Kross, tooling down the road, the coolest nigga in Cleveland. I even wore my pants backward like those little bastards. Talk about a pain in the ass if you have to piss. I fucked up two pairs of Guess jeans like that. The whole purpose of everything was to, of course, impress the women. I would break up relationships left and right. I'd cruise by a bus stop, and there would be a hot babe with her sorry-ass man who was too damn poor to have a car. My truck would be thunderbopping out her favorite song, I'd be there in my slick outfits. Who do you think would win those contests?

One evening I took a fine babe out to Red Lobster and then back to my apartment. After a couple hours or so, it was time to take her back home to Warrensville Heights, so we went out into the parking lot and SHIT WHERE THE FUCK IS MY GODDAMN TRUCK? I ran back into the apartment and called the Cleveland cops. A couple of cops got there pretty quickly. That seemed a bit odd. Why did they send two cops, and just what made them get there so quickly?

"Someone stole my goddamn truck," I pleaded to the officers.

"Yes, sir, we'll need your information," the one cop said.

"Yeah, sure, sure," I said. "Here's my license."

The officers looked at it, then at each other.

"Hold on a second, Mr. Ramsey," they said just before they

huddled off to the side, out of earshot. After maybe 30 seconds, they came back to me.

"Good news, Mr. Ramsey. We know where your truck is. And we know who took it."

"You're shittin' me! Damn, you guys work fast!" I was ecstatic that I was going to get my Blazer back just like that and the fucker who stole it was going to get his ass jailed. "When can I get it back?"

"It's down at the Master Plan Bar on Euclid. Your father would like for you to come get it. By the way, Mr. Ramsey," one of the cops said, "you might be able to lie to your father, but your father's bank statement don't lie to him."

OH FUCK. I knew what that meant. My old man would hang out at that bar, which was owned by one his fellow Masons. My truck was there, which meant he took it, which meant he probably had looked at his bank statement and medicated his pain with an entire bottle of Scotch. It was clear these cops knew that Dad wanted me to come dare try to get that truck. I knew that if I tried, that would probably be the end of me.

No way was I going down to that bar. Dad had something planned for me, and the cops were in on it. By now, the babe I was with was gettin' pretty antsy, so I asked the cops if they would take her home. They agreed. I then went back to my apartment and just shook. I had no car, and I had to get to work the next morning. The next few days I just hung around the apartment and laid low. Eventually I worked up enough nerve to string together a couple long RTA bus rides to get to Eli Wrecking to pick up my paycheck.

"When are you coming back to work?" they asked me when I arrived at the office.

"Got no car. Don't know."

"Well, you better get a car, or it's no job."

Ah, fuck 'em, I thought. I didn't care. But I had to do something. This was another fine mess I got myself into. I had already spent just about all the cash I took from Dad's account, so I couldn't just go buy another car. So I did what any suburban rich kid would do—I called Mom. I pleaded with Mom that I couldn't get to work without a car, and that a car was so important for me to learn responsibility, blah blah blah. A few days later I had myself a royal blue Buick Skylark. I'm sure it pained Dad to fork out for yet another car, but since it would keep me out of the house, it was a bargain.

We were then assigned the job of demolishing the old Stroh Brewery building on Quincy Avenue. The guys were all abuzz about this project, and at first I didn't know why. But I found out: It was copper. A poor man's get-rich-quick scheme. The guys were stripping all the copper out of the building. I wasn't about to pass on this easy money, so I loaded up my Buick Skylark with so much copper the car sagged and bottomed out. The job supervisor saw what was happening, and I was busted. The 300 pounds of scrap copper belonged to the company, not to me, and just like that I was fired. I wasn't the only guy helping himself to the copper; I just didn't have the brains to not do it in broad daylight. The other guys helped themselves to plenty of that shit, but they knew to do it at night. They knew the proper way to steal. I had no idea, either, what I was going to do with all that copper. A black kid showing up at a scrapyard with a car full of copper pipe screams THIEF. If I tried to sell it to a crackhead, he'd just crack my head and help himself to it. So I fucked up while fucking up.

Of course, because of Dad's connections, the company called him to report what had happened. Dad went into his usual tirade. This time there was no bailout. To teach me a lesson, as if I'd actually pay any attention to it, Dad stopped paying the rent on my apartment. Dad wasn't about to let me back in the house. I had fucked up one too many times, and Dad concluded there was only one option left.

MILITARY MAYHEM

Really I feel less keen about the Army every day. I think the Church would suit me better.

—Winston Churchill

Now THAT I HAD crashed and burned in two tries at college, at working in Florida, and at working for Dad, he determined there was only one option left for me: the military. Dad was an Air Force veteran, so he knew that lifestyle. If the military couldn't straighten me out, then nothing could.

Dad took me to the Army recruiting station on Euclid Avenue in East Cleveland. I listened to the recruiter go on and on about discipline, physical fitness, and how I could see the world for free. The Army seemed like a better deal than the Navy or the Marines. I didn't like the idea of floating around on a boat somewhere in the ocean, and Marines were just insane. The Air Force didn't appeal to me either. An Army guy will beat the shit out of you. An Air Force guy will just call the police. The recruiter probably thought he was a great salesman because I signed the papers right there. He was the pimp, I was the prostitute. The truth is that Dad made it very clear I was going to sign up that day, no questions asked. But as I was signing my life over to the Army, I was already thinking of ways to scam the system.

Three weeks later Dad drove me to the Federal Building downtown. There, I put my left hand on a Bible and was sworn in. We

The Army seemed like a good option for me—until they wanted to send me to a real war. Then I had to find a way to outsmart Uncle Sam. *(Charles Ramsey collection.)*

were told to say goodbye to our loved ones and get on the bus. There was no great emotional goodbye from Dad. He just huffed and said, "I'm sure I'll see you again soon." My pattern had already been well established.

As Dad headed back to his Caddy, I boarded the bus with the other fresh recruits. It was an all-night ride to Fort Leonard Wood, Missouri, which we referred to as "Fort Lost in the Woods." Hardly anyone got any sleep, as we spent the time talking and wondering what to expect and what surprises might be in store.

We arrived at 4:30 a.m., synchronized with the arrival of dozens of other buses from around the country. We found out very quickly that we were not in control. We didn't even have names anymore.

We were referred to as "soldier." In 20 minutes, we were off the bus, assigned to our squadrons, and standing at attention in the barracks.

Every day we did pushups till we threw up. And we learned never to refer to your weapon as a "gun." The rules were rigid and unforgiving. If one member of the unit fucks up, we all got fucked up. If someone didn't do their pushups right, we all had to start over. If someone did something out of order, we all had to start over. If some wuss whined that a drill was too hard, we all had to do it over again. This led to what we called "blanket parties." If one of the recruits in our unit fucked up and we all had to pay for it, we would sneak up on him in the middle of the night, pull his blanket down, and shove a pillow in his face. Then we would whale away on the asshole with whatever we could find—boots, canned goods, broomsticks—whatever we could get our hands on. The purpose of the blanket party was to send a message to the muthafucka that we didn't appreciate his fuckup. We covered his face with a pillow because we didn't want to leave any visible marks. During basic training we probably had a dozen or so blanket parties.

We all learned to be team players. I couldn't help but think to myself, *What have I gotten myself into? Have I met my match?* There was no choice but to follow the rules. The training not only got me prepared for service in the army; it got me prepared for time in the penitentiary.

After eight grueling weeks that would have made a Vince Lombardi training camp seem like a romp through pussyland, basic training was complete. There was a graduation ceremony, but my parents were definitely not in attendance. I did feel a sense of accomplishment when graduating. I had done something worthwhile without scamming the system. I'd gone from a rebellious prick who would do things half-ass to a finely tuned, dangerous, rebellious prick.

After basic training I continued on to Advanced Individual Training, or AIT, where I became a crane operator. I liked being a crane operator because it paid better than other vocations and I didn't have to shoot anybody. After eight weeks of AIT we were given the chance to pick where we wanted to go. We could go to China, Germany, or someplace stateside. I chose Germany because they make BMWs there, and that's my favorite car. If they could build a car like that, that must be a pretty cool place. We were herded onto a windowless military transport plane for an 18-hour flight from St. Louis to Kaiserslautern, Germany. K-town, as it was known, is in southwest Germany. About 50,000 Americans live in the city and surrounding area, making it the largest American population center outside U.S. territory. I loaded up a bunch of CDs and batteries, but somewhere over the Atlantic I ran out of both. We didn't sleep much on the flight. In fact, falling asleep invited trouble. One poor schmuck who fell asleep was rudely awakened by a cup of piss splashed in his face, which everyone, especially me, thought was funny as hell. After a refueling stop in London, we continued on to Ramstein Air Base. One of the first things I found at Ramstein was the local McDonald's. We know how much I enjoyed that. Another thing I quickly located was the red-light district in Frankfurt.

At 6:15 every morning we lined up in formation. We would hear announcements, orders, and instructions of what was going to happen that day. One morning, the drill sergeant went through his usual list of the day's activities and tagged on the end, ". . . and in one week this unit will be shipped out to assist in the liberation of Kuwait."

Holy fuck! Our unit was actually going to war?! Shit, this wasn't what I signed up for. I joined the Army to get away from the control of my old man and maybe learn to do something I could legally make money at, not to kill anyone. Yeah, I knew they were going to teach us how to efficiently kill people, but I never thought we'd *really* have to kill *real* people. Some of the guys in the unit were all gung-ho GI Joe about it; others weren't. Saddam Hussein didn't do anything to me, and I didn't give a shit about what happened to Kuwait. If the Iraqis were to ever come sailing up the Cuyahoga River, I'd be the first one there to blast the fuck out of them, all the while humming "Yankee Doodle Dandy," but going to Kuwait wasn't for defensive purposes. It was just a political war, nothing else. I wanted nothing to do with it. No fuckin' way was I going to have anything to do with a political war.

Unfortunately, when you're in the Army, you aren't given the option of whether or not you want to go to war. You go where they tell you. But I wasn't going. No way in fuckin' hell were they going to get me there. I couldn't exactly just turn in my resignation, so I had to come up with some way that I would be kicked out. But I didn't want to do something criminal because I didn't want to wind up in the stockade. If I just misbehaved or became all prickish they'd still drag my ass there. I had to come up with something, and come up with something fast. The Army has a long and bureaucratic process of dealing with assholes who've fucked up, so just doing stupid shit would take too long. I had already racked up scores of Article 15s—maybe 30 or 40—which are administrative ways of telling you that you fucked up. Too many Article 15s and they fuck *you* up. You can be confined to quarters, assigned "fatigue" duty, be docked pay, or be put on a bread and water diet. I, of course, was sanctioned in all the ways but the bread and water thing, but Article 15s aren't sufficient to get your ass kicked out.

I was a solid pain in the ass to the superior officers. My sergeant would have pulled his hair out except he was as bald as a cue ball. One of the "fatigue" duties I was once assigned was to strip and wax the barracks floor. That involved too much work, so I didn't bother with the stripping part. Then, instead of carefully measuring out the proper amount of wax for the floor area, I just dumped out the bottles all around and fired up the buffer. That floor shined like a full moon. The sergeant came by, said, "Good work, Ramsey," and tried to walk across the floor. He slipped and went down, whump! Flat on his ass bone. Another Article 15.

There were times when we would have combat exercises in the woods. While everyone was playing Army, I was sneaking out of the woods and into an awaiting car to take me to Frankfurt or wherever. Sometimes I would just head out to the road and hitch-hike. The Germans were very friendly and always glad to help out an American soldier. If a car of German dudes stopped to help me, I'd jump in and say, *"Wo sind die Huren?"* ("Where are the whores?") When everyone reported for formation after the exercises, they would notice I was missing. Since we subscribe to the "no man left behind" philosophy, the unit would be dispatched back into the woods to look for my sorry ass. Of course they would never find me. That got me enough Articles 15s to fill up the Sunday New York Times.

There was only one way to get out of this mess: make a pass at a lieutenant general. This was before the days of "don't ask, don't tell," and certainly before being gay had become so vogue. Being gay was still considered incompatible with military service. This would be my ticket home. It would mean a less than honorable discharge, but I didn't give a fuck. I wanted out.

At 6:15 the next morning, everyone fell into morning formation. Everyone except for me. I was issued another Article 15 by the commanding officer. I asked him to please suck my dick. That got me sent over to the first lieutenant. I repeated my request. That got me sent over to the Judge Advocate General's office; again, same request. Then the lieutenant colonel, the full colonel. They all warned me of the dire consequences of an Other Than Honorable discharge, and that I better shape up pretty quick. They weren't buying into the gay act. Then I was finally sent up to the lieutenant general, who tried a different tactic. Instead of threatening me with an other than honorable discharge, he tried convincing me that I may just be the type of person who could go far in the Army.

"Either you're an extremely rebellious person," the two-star said, "or you're just the type of guy we need." It was the lieutenant general's job to try to prevent me from getting kicked out, so he tried all the platitudes and attaboys he could think of. "Now, you really don't want to be discharged under these circumstances, do you?"

I sat there quietly. "Umm, please suck my dick."

With that, I was confined to the barracks, where I had an endless supply of cigarettes, a library of hundreds of movies at my disposal, and my meals brought to me. All I needed was a German whore. A similarly rebellious female soldier substituted just fine. After two weeks of confinement, one morning the sergeant came through the barracks door.

"Tomorrow morning you're flying outta here," he said in a defeated tone. "First to London, then to New Jersey, then to fucking Cleveland. You genius asshole."

I had done it. I had outsmarted the entire United States Army. I wasn't going to have to fight in any goddamn war. For me, an Other-Than-Honorable discharge took more brains and balls than a Harvard education. About 100,000 soldiers received such a discharge over the past 10 years, and all it means is that I don't get any VA benefits (don't need them) and I can't re-enlist or serve in the reserves (no problem there).

Although I was feeling pretty good about myself, I knew Dad would have a few things to say when I got home.

Don't for one second think that I'm some sort of anti-military kook. I was just anti-*me*-in-the-military. I was just too much of a self-centered asshole to fit in with that lifestyle. The guys and gals who have the guts and bravery to serve are true American heroes, from private to general.

Even though the Americans overwhelmed the Iraqis in the liberation of Kuwait, and casualties on our side were relatively light, several guys in my unit got their faces shot the fuck off.

When the plane landed in Cleveland, Dad was there to meet me. He had nothing to say to me, but I could tell the lava was rising to the surface. The volcano was emitting steam and ash. I could tell he was holding it in and that he didn't want to make a public spectacle. On the way home there were several things he could have said, none of them pleasant. He seemed focused on an earring I was sporting.

When we got home, I got out of my monkey suit, smacked my brother around, and raided the refrigerator. I watched TV, catching some "Cosby Show" and "Laverne and Shirley." I chilled and complimented myself for my brilliant scheme to get out of the army. I didn't think of what to do next. I didn't worry about it. Dad's money was my enabler, and once again I was the slickest nigga in the cotton field.

After a few hours of letting me chill, Dad zeroed in.

"What the fuck is that?" he bellowed, pointing at the diamond-studded earring in my ear. "You've been government property all this time. How the hell did they let you get a goddamn earring? Did you turn into some sort of sissy? Why didn't you just get a tattoo like normal GIs? Obviously you weren't cut out for the military. And I bet you're just fuckin' AWOL."

No argument there. The military life wasn't for me. I was glad to be out, and since I wasn't AWOL, I didn't give a fuck as to the status of my discharge. But there was another kink to the story. My parents thought I was just coming home for a Christmas visit. They had no idea I had been booted out of the Army. They kept asking me when I would have to return to Germany, and I kept putting them off. Eventually Dad looked in my duffle bag and saw my discharge papers. He didn't say anything. Then I asked Kevin to tell Dad for me. Dad wasn't surprised that I fucked up yet again.

*　　*　　*

"So what are you going to do next?" Dad hounded me. He knew I really had no answer, and he already had one for me. Dad had recently purchased a laundromat on Euclid Avenue and needed someone to babysit it. My job was to make sure no one broke into the machines and to clean up after heroin addicts. If a machine were to break down, I was supposed to go get Dad, who spent a good deal of time at the bar next door, which was owned by one of his fellow Masons. I wasn't supposed to fuck with the machines, something I liked to do—just let Dad know. I was doing something right, and legal, but certainly way underchallenging. Pay? I was living in Richmond Heights with room and board provided, and Dad thought that was quite enough. Dad had one standing rule: be in by his curfew. Now you can imagine just how well that sat with me. I was an adult, and nothing was going to stop me from doing my own thing. If I felt like hanging out for few days, that's exactly what the fuck I did. I needed to get away, and Dad wanted me out of the house. It was time to get the hell out of there.

I took whatever legitimate jobs I would come across. For a while I was a groomer and shit-pitching stablehand at Thistledown race-track, southeast of Cleveland. I would walk the horses around as a warm up, then walk them around as a cool down. I was making only minimum wage and not getting that many hours in. I found out that once they knew you and thought you were cool, management at Thistledown didn't mind if you spent the night sleeping in a stable. Being banned from home, that's where I stayed, sleeping amid the horseshit. After a few weeks of that, I became friends with another stablehand, who noticed my shit-lined accommodations.

He invited me to live with him in his house on Primrose, just off Euclid Avenue. I had a newer car now, a Mitsubishi Montero that I bought for 50 bucks off some crackhead on the street—strictly don't ask, don't tell. I realized that I had to do one of two things: rob people or sell drugs. Street robbery just wasn't my thing, so I chose the latter. I began hanging around on Euclid Avenue with the tough crowd—the scummy fuckers who would sell crack to your grandmother while in rehab. This was a profession in which I had the experience, and for which I had the balls.

East 105th and St. Clair corridor, in the heart of the Glenville neighborhood, was an open goldmine for drug dealers like myself. Plenty of despair, violence, and other sound reasons for people to turn to crack. It was easy work and big money—just my style.

My day would start at the Landmark Restaurant on St. Clair. They would open early in the morning, shut down in the middle of the day, then re-open in the evening. Perfect hours for the neighborhood drug dealers.

Driving down St. Clair Avenue, you might not notice a whole lot of suspicious activity. Mothers push baby strollers past dilapidated, century-old, dingy brick buildings. Some old-timers hanging out by the barbershop. A few fast food joints. Rusty cars rattling over a maze of potholes. You might not see a drug dealer, but they're there. Turn down any of the side streets. You won't have to go very far until you see a couple of dudes standing around looking like they've got nothing to do. They're doing plenty. If they're true professionals, the customers come to them. Only the amateurs try hanging on the main drags. That's where the cops will find them. Not only are the dealers waiting for their customers, they're keeping a watchful eye on their territory. If some punkass kid tries to break into the business by moving in on an established dealer's territory, he takes his life into his hands as if he were walking through a male grizzly bear's territory during mating season. Dealers will do what they have to do to protect their territory. I sure did. Yet, while on the street, I didn't carry a gun. Most dealers don't.

I would stand there on the street corner and sell $20 rocks by the boatload. Sometimes, though, I needed a place to hide so I could cut up some more rocks. I noticed a dark back porch on the back of a brick four-plex on the corner of Glenville and East 105th and determined it provided just the right amount of cover. I was working the street with my boy Tiny Man. I crouched down on the back porch and began to cut up some more of the Glenville Gold when a woman came out with a bag of garbage.

She saw me, dropped the bag, and let out a scream.

"Who the . . . get the hell out of here before I call the police!" she yelled, trembling.

"Whoa, easy there, it's cool, I'm cool, relax, baby," I said. I had no desire to do anything bad to this woman; I just needed her porch as a hiding place.

Seeing that I wasn't threatening her in any way, the woman calmed down a bit. Then Tiny Man came around back, and fortunately she recognized him from high school. That seemed to put her more at ease. I continued to talk to her, getting a little sweeter with my words. She began to talk a bit sweet to me. Her name was Rochelle. She was a nurse at a retirement center. And she was one fine babe.

Before I left, I told her I'd be back in a couple days. However, we had rather different perceptions of the reason why. I didn't view her at that time as a potential girlfriend. I saw her apartment as a strategic location for business purposes. It was right there in the high-speed lane of the high-traffic zone, the perfect place to store and sell crack. Rochelle made it clear she had no interest in smoking or selling that shit, so I didn't have to worry about her stealing it.

A couple days later I was doing business in the 'hood when I noticed Rochelle walking toward me. She kept coming, and walked up straight to my face.

"You told me you'd be back in a couple days. If you don't want me, tell me."

Hmm, I thought. This girl had no boyfriend, had a two-year-old son who needed some attention, and her car note was past due. To a crack dealer, this was a match made in heaven. In just a few days I managed to sweet talk her into letting me move in.

I had a good thing going. I was making plenty of tax-free cash, working as much or as little as I wanted, and was sleeping with a nice-looking woman. I took care of the house, doing a lot of the cooking and cleaning. I was not only one hell of a crack dealer, I was one hell of a house bitch. I liked taking care of her son, A.J. Every now and then I'd buy him a new video game. I kept a thriving business going. Customers knew to come to the bathroom window and rap once. There, I kept my inventory of crack, blunts, and a pistol.

I didn't conduct business out of the house all of the time. Sometimes I had to meet some people out on the street. You see, drug dealers think they're invisible. They think only the dumb fuckers get caught, and everyone else is a dumb fucker. You are untouchable. You are the man. You are the law. Reality, though, is that when you're a drug dealer, you're just an asshole in an upright position.

Sooner or later, it was bound to happen. I was out working when a cop car slowly cruised by. Experienced drug dealers know that you need to keep your inventory in your hand, not your pockets, so you can easily toss it away. Also, never run, because that of course is a dead giveaway that you're dealing. So when the cop car cruised by a second time, I casually dropped the crack rocks and kept walking like I owned the damn street. I thought I had positioned myself so that the cops wouldn't see the crack fall to the ground, but I was wrong.

"Think you're pretty smart, huh?" one cop said as he came at me from the front while the other cop grabbed my arms from the back. I knew it was useless to run or fight. I was busted.

They took me to the Sixth District Headquarters at East 152nd and St. Clair. It was a full house, and this was just a Thursday afternoon. You can imagine how many dudes would be there on a Friday or Saturday night. This being my first offense—well, more accurately, the first time I was caught—I was able to bond out in a matter of hours. Probation was going to be the most likely result, so I didn't sweat it. Seeing how quickly I was in and out, I still thought of myself as a pretty slick nigga.

I knew my dad had some cash in his safe, and that would come in very handy. (I had once before helped myself to a stack of business checks in his safe, being clever enough to take the checks at the bottom of the book so it was a while before he noticed anything.) My parents were away Christmas week of 1992, so I thought I'd just walk on in. I parked my car a few blocks away in an Arby's parking lot so no one on Donald Drive could say they saw anything. I walked the couple of blocks to my parents' house. All the doors and windows were locked. That was surprising. This was Richmond Heights, and usually they didn't lock everything up. I wondered if they had moved out, so I checked some mail in the mailbox. Yes, they still lived here. They must have just locked up because they were away for the week. I climbed up on the enclosed back porch because that would take me to their bedroom window. There was a screen over the window, so I jimmied at it for maybe two minutes until it finally popped off. Then I pushed up on the bedroom window. Success! It wasn't locked. I had it up maybe an inch or so when all of a sudden this ear-splitting siren blasted away right above my head. The noise knocked me backward. SHIT!

This place was alarmed! I better get outta here fast. I picked myself up and turned to get off the porch roof and then, FUCK! There were the Richmond Heights Police, cold steel pointed at me. Once again, Dad was one step ahead of me in our never-ending chess match. He figured I might try to do something brilliant like this, so in my absence he'd had both live and silent alarms installed.

I was taken to the station and processed in, then taken into an interrogation room. While just gazing around I noticed the ceiling. It was a simple acoustic-tile drop ceiling. That meant you could push up on a tile and find space above the ceiling. It might not be a lot of space, and the hardware that holds the tiles in place isn't very sturdy, but for this crafty nigga the opportunity was just too good to pass up. The Richmond Heights jail wasn't exactly a maximum-security facility, so I looked for an opportunity to make my move. When the coast was clear, I popped up a tile and pulled myself up and into the space above the ceiling, neatly replacing the tile. I moved slowly through the space, using the crawling technique I learned in the Army. Slowly I slithered quietly along, feeling my way through the darkness until I felt a wall. Damn, couldn't get out that way. I pulled a tile up a bit to let a little light in, only to see that there were solid walls on all sides. No way to get out.

Just then, the two cops came back in the interrogation room. "Shit, where did he go?" one of them said. But the other cop was already on to me.

"Well," he said nice and loud, "I guess we'll just have to take our guns out and start shooting at the ceiling."

Whoa, that's all I needed to hear. "Yo, officer, ugh, hey, um, that won't be necessary," I said. I wanted to make sure they knew I was in the ceiling because if I just pulled up one of the tiles and poked my head out they might think it was duck season and that I was Daffy Duck. My ass is just as black as his. I slowly pulled a tile off, then dangled my lanky leg so that if they shot at me that's all they'd hit. They grabbed my leg and pulled me down and cuffed me. I was put into a cell for a short while, then they came in and told me that I was now considered an escape risk. I was going to be transferred to the big jail downtown.

I was rather proud of myself. This jail couldn't hold this bad nigga! No way! I was sent down to the county jail at the Justice Center downtown. There, I got to mingle with first-rate assholes, rapists, and murders. Burglarizing my parents' home didn't exactly measure up to who's-the-baddest-muthafucka-in-the-house standards.

Things got a bit worse not long after I arrived. Remember, I had left my car—my $50, no-questions-asked car—in the Arby's parking lot before I tried to break into the house. Eventually the car was towed. And I had left my driver's license in the fucking car. So in addition to being charged with burglary, I was now charged with receiving stolen property. Another case of fucking up while fucking up.

I was let out of jail pending my sentencing hearing. While waiting for that hearing, I got busted again, this time for selling drugs. When I finally got my day in court, Dad was there.

"Mr. Ramsey," the judge said, "your father is here to speak on your behalf."

What a lucky break. If anyone had the connections to get me out of this mess, it was the old man. I smiled as he stood up to give his speech.

"Your honor," Dad said, "I want you to give this nigger the maximum. I'm sick and tired of his shit, and I don't want to see him around Richmond Heights again. I've tried everything I could to set him straight, but he's just too much of a dumbshit. He needs prison time, lots of it."

"Well, um, Mr. Ramsey, the most I can give your son is 18 months."

"Not fuckin' enough," the old man ranted on. "I'll pay to have him kept longer. He needs at least five years."

The judge gave me a 12-month sentence and a six-month sentence, which ran concurrently. I was sent to the Lorain Correctional Institution in Grafton, Ohio.

While doing my time, Rochelle and I kept in touch. "I hope you remember this address," she told me. A year later, I did. I was released and put on a bus back to Cleveland. I got off with nothing more than the clothes on my back. I walked east on St. Clair Avenue—some 90 city blocks from the bus station—then trudged up East 105th Street to the brick building at 105th and Glenville. There on the back porch was Rochelle. I was now home.

DOMESTIC UNTRANQUILITY

Marriage is neither heaven nor hell, it is simply purgatory.
—Abraham Lincoln

ROCHELLE'S MOTHER KEPT PUSHING for us to get married. She knew what I did for a living—hell, everyone did—but she was more concerned with the image of her daughter co-habitating out of wedlock. I had a good little setup going—I helped out with A.J., bought him video games and such. Sometimes, though, I smoked a bit too much weed while watching him and I'd forget he was there. But Rochelle's mother kept pressing the issue.

"Let me tell you something, bitch," I snarled while poking a finger in her face. "I'm going to take care of her and her kid. I don't give a fuck about what you think." That certainly wasn't the most polite way to talk to your future mother-in-law, but in the black culture she had stepped way over her bounds. Yes, I was an asshole.

Finally, Rochelle and I decided to go ahead and get married. So on Valentine's Day, 1995, we walked into the office of Judge Larry Jones, whom Dad had helped get elected. It was a very low-key affair. Dad was the best man.

"Rochelle is either one hell of a woman, or one hell of a dumb woman to marry a dumb nigga like you," Dad said with his usual charm. In reality, though, he was right.

"Hi, Chucky. Good to meet you," Judge Jones said.

"Howya doin,' Larry," I responded.

"Chucky!" Mom admonished me as she whacked me on the back of the head. "You address him as 'Your Honor.'"

The ceremony was quick, simple, and civil. We then went back to my parents' house, where we actually had a cake. That was the extent of the reception. Rochelle and I stayed the night in my old room. Considering that she started the day in the ghetto of 105th and Glenville, this was like the Ritz-Carlton to her. The next day, a Wednesday, we got up and went to work—she at the retirement home, me back in the maze of streets along St. Clair Avenue. I continued my life as a drug dealer, and she resumed her role as a Mafioso wife. As long as the bills were getting paid, A.J. looked after, and the house clean, she didn't care what the fuck I was doing. I wouldn't have cared what the fuck she thought if she did care, anyway.

*   *   *

On December 13, 1997, we welcomed Ashely Nichae Maraih Ramsey to the world. We moved into a triplex in Cleveland Heights. We lived on the third floor, with Rochelle's mother living on the second floor. The deal was that Rochelle's mother would look after the kids while I worked. I did whatever odd jobs I could do, as well as doing work for the landlord for reduced rent. But selling drugs was the fastest, easiest money I could make.

One day Rochelle's mother got into some sort of altercation with a woman down the street. This woman yelled at all of us that she was going to call her grandson, who was going to come down and straighten things out. So Tiny Man and I sat on the front porch, waiting for this grandson to arrive. Between Tiny Man and myself (we're both about 6 feet 5) this grandson, or anybody for that matter, struck no fear in our minds. Besides, we had a .38 special sitting between us just in case we needed a little backup.

A car pulled up, and five kids jumped out. Yes, they were kids. Maybe 17, 18. Tiny Man and I looked at each other, and then looked at these kids. Their numbers didn't intimidate us, but I'm sure our collective size scared the fuck out of them. We really didn't want to beat the shit out some kids, and they were smart enough not to fuck with us, so, instead of something ugly, we began to just hang and chill. We talked about politics, religion, and music.

Turns out these kids were actually the rap group Bone Thugs-n-Harmony. This group, from Cleveland, were still in their teens when they hit it big in late 1993. They had a rather non-typical style of rap, combining rapid-fire gangsta lyrics with touches of spot harmony. Kinda like Dr. Dre meets The Carpenters. They were discovered by former N.W.A rapper Eazy-E, and he signed them to a record deal with Ruthless Records in 1993. They were a quick big hit. They are the only rap group that worked with 2Pac, the Notorious B.I.G., Eazy-E, and Big Pun.

I began to hang with those guys, and eventually they offered me a job as a security guard on their cross-country tours. I jumped at the opportunity. Rochelle thought differently. She didn't like the idea of her husband criss-crossing the country with a band of teenagers who weren't exactly traveling bible salesmen. But I took the job and traveled all over with the group. They treated me very well, paid me well, even treated me to a Hollywood shopping spree.

During one break in the touring, Rochelle and I argued over my job constantly and, as a result, I wound up with domestic violence charge #1. That came in February 1997. I pled no contest but was found guilty. While waiting to be sentenced, I fucked up again and got arrested for domestic violence a second time. When it came time to be sentenced for the first case, I didn't bother to show. I fuckin' didn't care. The cases were then consolidated in August 1998. I did six months at the Cleveland House of Correction in Warrensville Heights.

While I was in the workhouse, Dad helped out Rochelle. When I

Wedding day, Feb. 14, 1995. Dad said Rochelle was either one hell of a woman or one hell of a dumb woman to marry me.
(*Charles Ramsey collection.*)

got out, he told me she wanted me to come back, but not quite yet. I stayed at my parents' house for a month or so, then went back to the apartment with her. On the surface we were semi-happy, but in reality we were totally dysfunctional.

In January 2003, things took a final turn for the worse. I had been suffering with sciatic nerve pain in my back. Rochelle mentioned that to my parents, but Dad didn't believe it.

"Pinched nerves happen to guys who work for a living," Dad said. "Chucky don't work. He sells drugs."

Dad was correct about my occupation, but it was still true that I had one fuckin' ass pinched nerve, to the point that I had to lie on the floor just so in order to not scream in pain. I was lying on the floor, playing "Madden Football," when the phone rang. I answered it in my usual professional manner.

"What the fuck do ya want?"

"Hi. Is this Mr. Ramsey?" an unfamiliar female voice timidly asked.

"Yea. Who's dis?"

"You don't know me, but your wife knows my husband. I mean, they know each other too much. Way too much."

"What the fuck are you talkin' 'bout?"

"Your wife is enrolled at Tri-C, right?" (That's the community college where Rochelle was taking classes.)

"Uh, yeah."

"And you're suffering with a sciatic nerve, right?"

"Uh, yeah again."

"And you've been taking a lot of pain pills to deal with it. Probably too many."

"How the fuck you know dis shit?"

"I overheard my husband talking on the phone to someone last night. He's also enrolled at Tri-C. I heard him giggling with someone about how her husband was probably going to die because he was taking too many pills to deal with his sciatica. I checked the outgoing call list and here's your number. I confronted him and beat her name out of him."

"Why that goddamn bitch. I'll be ready for her when she gets home."

As I lay there on the floor, a burning rage welled up inside of me. The extreme back pain combined with this news was just too much to take. Soon Rochelle came back from the store, along with my mother. They walked through the door, and I leapt like a mountain lion. Or at least I tried to. I hit the floor, writhing in so much fucking pain, but I was determined to kill her.

"You goddamn bitch!" I yelled, half out of rage, half from excruciating pain. "I know who you've been fuckin', you whore. I'm gonna fuckin' kill you!" I lunged for her again, but my back jolted me like I had been tasered. I grabbed the edge of a table and pulled myself up, then flailed away as I hit the floor again.

"You goddamn bitch. You fuckin' goddamn bitch!"

Again I struggled to my feet, my back on fire, and lunged at her again. This time Mom stepped between us and hit me with a two-finger eye poke just like Moe so artfully did on "The Three Stooges" all those years. It was a direct hit. I hit the floor again, now with my eyes hurting like a son-of-a-bitch as well.

"I'm gonna kill you, bitch. I'm gonna fuckin' kill you." I meant it, too. Had I not had this goddamn pinched nerve, I no doubt would have killed her. I was that much out of control.

Meanwhile, Rochelle made it to the phone and dialed 911. The 911 operator heard me yelling in the background. The cops came, and I cooked up some bullshit story about how some dude in red sweatpants broke in and I was just trying to defend us. They didn't buy it, and they hauled me off while I screamed and yelled like an eight-year-old girl who just saw her first spider.

Because I had two prior convictions, I was charged with felony domestic violence with prior conviction. The judge gave me eight months at the Lorain Correctional Institution, but I was transferred to the Marion Correctional Institution in Marion, Ohio. I became inmate 44972.

That summer I didn't hear anything from Rochelle. No letters, no phone calls, no visitors, nothing from anybody. But in September I did hear from Rochelle, in the form of a divorce filing. I knew I had been a first-class scumbag, and I can't blame her for wanting out. She had taken me back time and time again. Now she finally wised up. When I got the copy of the divorce complaint, it cut me deep. I loved that woman. I was crazy about her. But I put her through hell. For so long and for so many times I was able to weasel my way out of responsibility for my own stupid-ass acts. This was one of the few times it caught up with me, and certainly this was the most painful. Even more painful than prison itself.

*   *   *

Prison changes you. When you choose to live life at 1,000 miles per hour with no airbags, that's where you wind up. They call it "corrections" and "rehabilitation" but it is neither. You go in as a fuckup and come out as a desensitized fuckup. You don't come out as a model citizen. I did conduct business while in prison. The same things that happen on the street happen in prison, just without women. I pretty much stayed out of trouble, never getting into a fight or major confrontation of any type. But that's not because I wasn't willing to. In prison, the concept of "peace through strength" rules. You needed to make it clear by your look, your words, and your actions that you have no problem knocking the fuck out of anyone who would cause you trouble. If that message was clear and you stayed out of other's people's business, you were pretty much left alone. Some stupid fucks just didn't get the idea. They would get their heads split open sometimes for major issues (like if you owed someone money) or for minor issues—like if you slept too close to someone who didn't like you. Stupid fuckers would try to reason with bad fuckers by pointing out that the beds were bolted to the floor and couldn't be moved. That would get their head bashed into a steel bedpost. If a bad fucker said you were sleeping too close, that meant *you* move, asshole.

When my discharge day, or "out-day" as we called it, arrived, I was processed out and put into a van at about 11 a.m. The van took us to the Greyhound station in Columbus, where we were each given $75 in cash and a bus ticket home. I didn't know where home was for me anymore. My parents didn't want me around their house, and certainly Rochelle knew better than to take another chance on me. As the bus rolled its way up Interstate 71 north for the two-hour trip to Cleveland, I thought of the friends I'd left behind at Marion. I'm not saying for a second that I was sorry to leave them—hell, no way did I want to spend another goddamn minute in that rat hole—but I couldn't help but to feel bad for so many of those dudes who had spent the majority of their adult lives locked up. No hope. Nothing to look forward to. The mundane life of a cold, smelly prison was their only existence.

The bus pulled into the Greyhound station at East 13th and Chester. I stepped off, again wearing all my worldly possessions, and looked around. There was my brother, Kevin.

"Dad told me you'd be here," he said. While I was glad that someone was there for me, another screwy chapter in my crazy life was about to unfold.

Kevin told me he had a place for me to stay and had lined up a job for me. Fantastic. Kevin had become somewhat of a real estate mogul. He would buy, sell, and rent houses around town. He hooked me up with a guy named Perry who had a contract with the Department of Housing and Urban Development. I would work for this guy cleaning out foreclosed houses. Kevin let me stay in a house on Sylvania Drive. That worked out well until one morning there was a bang on the door. There stood the housing inspector, flanked by three or four sheriff's deputies.

"You have three days to vacate this house."

Well, apparently Kevin didn't actually own the house.

Fortunately, Perry offered me an apartment at East 108th and Union in a building he used for storage. We worked from Youngstown to Toledo, clearing out and cleaning up foreclosed homes. One nice perk of the job was that anything we found in the house we could keep. I found all sorts of things—futons, plasma TVs, DVD players, Louis Vuitton knockoffs, luggage, diamonds, porn videos, and even a mink coat, which I sold for $700. Perry would be surprised how fast the crew I was on always finished a job. Nearly all the houses we cleaned out had no electricity, so most of the guys relied on brooms, mops, and the like. But I knew how to pop open the electric meter and turn the power on, so everywhere our crew went we could use vacuum cleaners and power tools.

I enjoyed this job, and it kept me out of trouble. I went to work every day and just minded my own business. This allowed Dad and me to keep out of each other's hair. I wasn't living big, but I was making it on my own. But after three years or so, business began to slow, and I knew I would have to move on. I called my friend Leron, who lived down the street, and asked him if they were hiring where he worked, a fine restaurant named Moxie, in Beachwood. (Moxie is where billionaire Al Lerner signed the deal to bring the Cleveland Browns back in 1999.) Leron hooked me up with the executive chef, who asked me to start the next day. I learned how to prepare food to the point that I became a kitchen assistant—I would prepare the food most of the way and the chef would just finish it. This was in addition to being a dishwasher, or "ceramic technician" as they preferred to call us.

*   *   *

I managed to stay out of trouble for five years.

Eventually I looked around to see if maybe I could improve my job situation. I struck a deal with the owner of a deli and bakery in Lyndhurst. I worked in the kitchen and got a place to stay in the owner's house, as well. It became evident to me that the restaurant was struggling, and I knew my job and place to stay were at risk. I called a friend of a friend, Sherman, who I knew once lived in a boarding house on Cleveland's west side. Sherman gave me the name and number of the landlord. I called the guy, and we met up at 2203 Seymour Avenue.

When I walked into the place, I could see and smell black mold everywhere. The furniture was circa 1962; the carpet was green and fuzzy like a worn-out tennis ball. The kitchen consisted of a Frigidaire refrigerator, which I believe was white at some time, along with a microwave oven and a George Foreman grill. No stove or oven. But from what Sherman told me, as long as the rent was paid and you didn't destroy the place, the landlord didn't give a crap what you did. And at $75 a week, it was affordable.

I was still working at the deli way over on the east side of town, so I had to deal with a very long commute. I had no car. My license had been suspended years ago, and I didn't bother getting that problem fixed. So every day I took the bus up West 25th Street to the RTA Rapid Transit station there by the West Side Market. From there I took the rapid transit train seven miles to University Circle, where I would catch the 9x bus to Lyndhurst. It was a three-hour trek each way.

The commute was getting to me rather quickly. My friend Andrew was working at this new restaurant downtown called Hodge's. I asked if they were hiring, and he told me to come on in. I went in to Hodge's, located at 668 Euclid Avenue, mistakenly doing so during the lunch hour. I had to wait around for about an hour or so, but then Andrew came out, handed me an application and the other paperwork, and asked me when I could start. I wanted to be fair to my current boss, so I said two weeks. Andrew told me they needed me tomorrow, so that was it. I was hired without an interview, without any reference check.

*   *   *

Dad could no longer hold me back. School administrators could no longer hold me back. The Army could no longer hold me back. Crack dealin' could no longer hold me back. Prison could no longer hold me back. Hell, even my own stupidity couldn't hold me back. Having finally outgrown my trouble-making days, I thought I'd found my niche in the world. I could be an ordinary guy—go to work, pay my rent, have a nice dinner, enjoy the company of nice women.

What I didn't know is that my plans were good as fucked. I was living mere feet away from one of the most horrific crime scenes ever and one of the most fucked up monsters to ever prowl the planet. Not a clue, bro. Not a fuckin' clue.

I'd been living on Seymour Avenue for just a week or so when I came home one night after a long shift at Hodge's. I cranked up the music and indulged in some self-medication. It was probably 2 a.m. or so when there was a knock on the door. It was my new next-door neighbor, Ariel Castro.

"Now I know you just moved in here," he said, "but you gotta understand that I drive a school bus. I have to get up in a couple of hours."

"Say no more," I said. "I apologize." I turned the music down. The last thing I wanted to do was develop a bad reputation in my new neighborhood.

THE GIRLS

When news broke that Amanda Berry, Gina DeJesus and Michelle Knight were freed from a decade of captivity on Seymour Avenue in May, a city—and a nation—was captivated. It was that captivation, culminating in the eventual demise of captor Ariel Castro, that led U.S. editors and news directors to choose 'Missing Women Found' as one of the nation's 10 biggest news stories of 2013 in an Associated Press poll released Sunday.
—Northeast Ohio Media Group

MICHELLE, AMANDA, AND GINA all have stories very different, yet the same. Amanda and Gina teamed up on a book, and Michelle decided to do one on her own. While I know quite a bit about what went on among the girls, I will let them tell their own stories. From what I understand, there will be some significant conflict in the girls' stories. I am not going to take a position on whose story is most accurate. I honestly don't know. All I will say is that I hope everyone gives all three, actually four, girls the same love and affection you all have shown me. What they went through is something few people could ever comprehend, or survive.

The only one I've had personal contact with since is Michelle. By chance, we live very close to each other, and Thanksgiving 2013 I saw her walking her dog. I walked up to her and said, "Hi, Michelle." She looked up at me and said, "Oh, hi. It's good to meet you finally." It wasn't a dramatic meeting, just a low-key meeting similar to that of old friends.

Michelle was Ariel Castro's first victim. She was 21 at the time. She was walking to an appointment with social services about a custody issue concerning her young son on August 22, 2002, when she lost her way. She walked in the door of the Family Dollar store on Clark Avenue (the same place where those Puerto Rican kids would later try to sell me those fake pit bulls the day of the rescue). She asked for directions, and standing next to her was that fuckin' bastard Ariel. He told her he knew where she needed to go and would be glad to take her. Michelle recognized him as the father of one of her friends, Emily. So with no hint of what was in store, she gladly accepted the fateful ride. The next day, her mother Barbara reported her missing.

Instead of driving her to the social services office, Ariel drove her to his house, where Michelle fell for the old "come look at the puppies" trick. Fooled by Michelle's 4-foot-7 stature, Ariel thought he had snagged a 13-year-old. When he found out her real age, he was outraged. The bastard chained her by her neck and waist to a pole in the basement. Michelle said she heard many people come over to the house, but Ariel would stuff her mouth with a sock and duct tape it shut. She wished for death, but thoughts of her son kept her going. Sixteen months later, she would get company. By that time, authorities had believed that Michelle had simply run away, and thus she became the "forgotten" victim.

Amanda Berry was one day short of her 17th birthday on April 21, 2003. She worked at the Burger King near West 117th Street and Lorain. After her shift she was going to walk home when someone offered to give her a ride. Hating to be seen in her Burger King uniform, she gladly accepted. According to an eyewitness, it was more than a someone. There were three someones. One of them was described as a pudgy Cuban-looking person.

After a year of vigils, tearful pleas, and dead ends, Amanda's mother, Louwana, contacted "The Montel Williams Show," where

Amanda Berry, Gina DeJesus, and Michelle Knight in photos taken near the time of their disappearances. *(FBI)*

they arranged a TV show meeting with psychic Sylvia Browne. Big mistake.

Sylvia was just another skanky pseudo-psychic who exploited tragedies to make a buck. Louwana was a desperate mother looking for whatever fragment of information to either give her hope or closure. She got neither.

"Can you tell me if they'll ever find her? Is she out there?" Louwana asked.

"She's—see, I hate this, when they're in water, I just hate this. She's not alive, honey," the damn bitch told her. Supposedly a short, stocky Burger King customer in his 20s wearing a red fleece coat killed Amanda on her birthday, and a black-hooded jacket she was wearing now covered with the killer's DNA was in a dumpster, Sylvia said while piling the shit higher.

I can see how desperate people might fall prey to charlatan psychics like Sylvia Browne. But the rest of you "sane" people—I don't get how you can be suckered by psychics and readers and what not. They're all as phony as a three-dollar bill. You can imagine how Louwana's heart sank. The heartbreak went from the unimaginable to the physical. Louwana's health took a turn for the worse, and she eventually died of heart failure, never knowing her daughter's true fate.

Some furious Twitter and Facebook users called Sylvia a "grief vampire" and a "hunch-backed harpy," among other things. They were way too kind.

This wasn't the first time that bitch fucked up and put a family through unnecessary torment. In 2003, she incorrectly told the parents of Shawn Hornbeck, a missing 11-year-old boy, that their son was dead, and that his body could be found near "two jagged boulders," ABC News reported. Nearly four years later, Shawn was later found living with his kidnapper Michael Devlin, 60 miles from his home in Missouri.

Sylvia died on November 20, 2013, obviously failing to predict her own death. For Louwana's sake, find Sylvia's grave and piss on it.

Gina DeJesus, who had just turned 14 a week before, started to walk home from school on April 2, 2004. She was with her good friend Arlene Castro. Arlene was Ariel's daughter. Gina gave Arlene 50 cents so Arlene could call her mother and see if she could go home with Gina. Arlene's mother said no, that she needed to come straight home. So the two friends headed their separate ways. That's when Gina came across Ariel, who offered her a ride home. Gina probably felt very secure accepting a ride home from her good friend's father, right there on a busy street in broad daylight.

But of course, Gina didn't make it home. She was taken to Ariel's house and tossed in the prison with the other two captives. Gina, being the youngest of the victims, had the most youth robbed from her.

SEYMOUR AVENUE

THE COMMUNITY AROUND SEYMOUR Avenue was tight-knit and self-sufficient. Almost everything you might need could be found within walking distance. Everyone there knew each other's business. There weren't very many secrets. This is why I speculate—not accuse, but speculate—that *somebody* on that street had to know that *something* was going on in Ariel's house. Ariel obviously was a genius monster, but to carry out the so-far crime of the century for 12 goddamn years without anyone knowing just stretches the limits of believability.

But I'm not saying it's impossible.

Ariel was, at least on the outside, the ideal neighbor. He went to work every day, cut his grass, brought his garbage cans in, fixed his cars, painted his porch, and kept to himself.

One of the guys in the neighborhood, Juan Perez, told ABC News, "Everyone thought he was a great guy."

I can look back with 20/20 hindsight and realize there were several clues that something really odd was going on.

When we had those barbeques, Ariel would always do his cooking and bring it over to the neighbors' houses. Neighbors never came onto his property.

I had noticed that Ariel's windows were boarded up or covered up with plastic. There were no air conditioning units, so you can only imagine how stifling that place would be in the summer. When I asked some of the neighbors why Ariel's house was boarded up in the summer with no air conditioning, they told me that's just a Puerto Rican thing, that he liked everything *muy caliente*. Well, I've got plenty of African DNA in me but I would at least want some ventilation in my house. No one ever said, "Hmm, that is odd."

In the winter, my roomie Shultzie and I once noticed that one of the windows was constantly iced over while others weren't. I wouldn't be surprised if that bastard was heating the rooms he was using and freezing the rooms where the girls were kept.

I remember Ariel's daughter Angie coming over to the house several times. She was one fine-lookin' babe. I kept my distance since she was Ariel's daughter and the man code made her ineligible for me. But when Angie would come by, Ariel would take forever to answer the front door. He would then give her some sort of hand signal to go around the back.

Many times Ariel would see me outside and call me over. "Hey, I've got this leftover food here—you want it?" he would ask. It looked good to me, so I gladly accepted, appreciative of his generosity. But it turns out he wasn't being generous—he was using me as a guinea pig. He would sometimes have the girls cook for him, and fearing they might be trying to poison him, he figured he'd better try it out on the nigga next door.

There were dots there, just never connected.

Ariel wasn't the only secret madman of Seymour Avenue.

After the rescue, the authorities checked out all the neighbors up and down the street. They discovered Elias Acevedo Sr., a registered sex offender who had failed to report his whereabouts to authorities.

Turns out he had raped and murdered his 30-year-old neighbor, Pamela Pemberton, in 1994, and then killed Christina Adkins, a pregnant 18-year-old who disappeared near Seymour in 1995, and stuffed her into a manhole.

While he was in jail, DNA evidence linked him to a rape that had occurred near where Pam's body was found. He then confessed to the rape and murder of both women, and was sentenced to 445 years in prison without the possibility of parole. That means this rescue has resulted in the solving of five kidnappings and two murders. Not bad for a toothless dishwasher. For my next act, I think I'll go find Jimmy Hoffa.

Elias' crimes were 20 years old. This again leads to the question: How could *two* sicko madmen with horrific secrets dating back 20 years and living on the same block keep all those crimes quiet from the rest of the we-know-your-business community?

According to an eyewitness, on the day she was taken Amanda got into a car with three men when she thought she was getting a ride home from Burger King. Who were these men, and what did they know and when?

I knew that to fit in with the neighborhood I shouldn't embarrass the culture or say anything stupid about it. In a way, I tried to join in. I learned a little Spanish and enjoyed the cookouts and street fiestas. (I must say, there are few things hotter than Puerto Rican women doing the merengue.)

Often I am asked, "What do you think would have happened if Ariel had come back while you were breaking down his door?" I can't say for sure, but I wouldn't have been surprised if it had gone something like this: Ariel would have pulled up in his driveway, seen me kicking in his door, and would have said, "What the fuck are you doing?" I would have turned around and Ariel would have been standing there, arms folded, and a dozen other of his fellow countrymen would have stood there with him. Ariel would have told Amanda, "Get back in the house, bitch, and I'll deal with you later." He would have told the others, "Oh, that's my girlfriend." Three or four big guys would have grabbed me by the arms and dragged me around the corner to the overgrown cemetery between Seymour and Wade. One of them would have put a gun to the back of my head and pulled the trigger. Another would have plunged a needle in my arm and shot me full of heroin. Another would have dropped a crack pipe in my hand. Three months later some poor schmuck walking his dog through the cemetery would have stumbled across my bony ass, seen the crack pipe in my moldy hand and would have thought, "just another fuckin' crackhead getting what he deserved" as he helped himself to my Air Jordans. It never would have made the news. And his dog would have pissed in my empty eyehole. And the girls would still be locked up in Ariel's house.

Sometimes, after a long night out drinking, I would stumble down Seymour Avenue back to my house. I would be too tired or lazy to make it into my own bathroom so I would take a leak right there on the basement window of Ariel's house. Good God, who knows how many times I essentially pissed right above those girls' heads? I fuckin' feel like shit now for doing that.

Here's something I heard among friends, and let me say I heard this but I didn't see it so I don't know if it's true. Some say a disguised Amanda and Jocelyn, who was born Christmas Day 2006, would walk to the corner store every so often. Others said they saw women in Ariel's backyard every once in a while. I never saw the three girls in the backyard, and my house was about five inches away from Ariel's. But like I said before, I did see Jocelyn in the backyard playing with those two greasy dogs, and I just thought she was his granddaughter. So while I can say I only saw Jocelyn in the backyard a few times, I can't tell you what other people saw when they say they think they saw Amanda and the others in disguise. It's possible. But if the girls were let out at times, why didn't anyone yell for help?

ARIEL

He's dead to me.

—Angie Gregg, Ariel's daughter

IF NO ONE IN the neighborhood knew what was going on, they weren't alone in being fooled. Ariel fooled the City of Cleveland, too. In January of 2004, Ariel was substituting on a school bus route that takes ADHD kids to Wade Park Elementary for a couple hours. He picked up two kids, and when he arrived at the school, he let one of the kids off, then drove the bus over to a Wendy's. When he got there, he noticed the boy was still on the bus. Ariel just yelled, "Lay down, bitch," and proceeded to go inside the restaurant, leaving the boy alone. Ariel eventually came out, and after driving around for a while, finally got the kid to the school. By then, the program for that day was over, so the kid was sent back home on Ariel's bus. The kid's grandmother reported the incident to the Cleveland cops, who went over to Ariel's house to interview him. Apparently the cops didn't notice anything suspicious. The whole matter was closed a month later for insufficient evidence.

Each morning during the school year Ariel would be out the door about 7 a.m., and would return midday, parking his bus in front of my house or his. Then sometimes he'd do something that, in retrospect, of course, showed that he had some serious issues. In between his bus runs, sometimes he'd come back out in a new outfit and then put this lifelike mannequin, complete with slanted eyes and a wig, in the back of one of his cars and zip off. Then he'd

Ariel Castro, one of the most notorious criminals in Cleveland history—and my next-door neighbor. *(Cuyahoga County Jail)*

come back, go out on the p.m. run, and get back late afternoon to early evening. Oftentimes he would then go out in the evening to gig with one of his bands.

Here's something I found out that's a bit telling. Since 2012, during the time the girls were held, the police were called out to that section of Seymour Avenue over 160 fuckin' times. Some neighbors claimed they called the cops because they heard screams of "get off of me" and a baby crying or heard pounding sounds coming from Ariel's house. Yet, since the cops didn't see anything, they just left.

On the Internet there's video of an encounter between super villain Ariel Castro and Cleveland cop Jim Simone, who was nicknamed "Super Cop." Ariel was zipping along south on Pearl Road near Denison Avenue on one of his motorcycles with the license plate turned sideways, a common tactic for someone who wants to make it difficult for law enforcement to casually run his plate. Officer Simone, who has something like 10,000 arrests to his credit and has shot 11 people in the line of duty, five of them fatally, followed him to a Shell station where Ariel had pulled in to fill up. Ariel was visibly nervous as Supercop approached. Their encounter was captured on Officer Simone's dash cam.

Simone: Let me see your driver's license.

Castro: Excuse me?

Simone: Let me see your driver's license, please.

Castro: What's wrong?

Simone: First off, your plate's improperly displayed. It has to be displayed left to right, not upside down or sideways. The law says you have to be able to read it from behind.

Castro: I just got it out so—

Simone: Where's your motorcycle endorsement?

Castro: That I don't have.

Simone: Another question is, why you riding it then? You don't have a helmet on, you don't have a license to operate it—you're setting yourself up to be arrested. Is that what you want?

Castro: No, sir, I don't want that.

Simone: The law says you have to be able to read 'em from behind. These plates don't belong to this bike, do they? What year Yamaha is this?

Castro: This is 2000.

Simone: Where's the Harley if the plates are gone?

Castro: Oh, the Harley. I sold it and I traded it in for this one.

Simone: Well, Ariel, you keep getting deeper and deeper.

Castro: I know, but I just got off work. I'm a school bus driver. And . . .

It's certainly a good thing that Supercop Jim, who is now with the Sheffield Lake Police Department, didn't arrest Ariel then and there. Does anyone think that bastard would have said something to the effect of "Um, somebody needs to stop by my house and feed a few girls locked up in the basement"? Had he been put away for anything more than a few days, we all know how this story would have ended. Supercop Jim issued Ariel a couple of citations and made him push the motorcycle back home.

"Well, actually, he was arrestable," Officer Simone told CNN. "He didn't have a license to operate a motorcycle, and normally I would arrest people for that, but he was very polite, and he explained to me he was a school bus driver, so if I had physically arrested him and towed his bike, there was a good possibility he might have lost his job as school bus driver. So I took that into consideration and I made him—I gave him a couple of tickets—I made him push the bike all the way home."

Asked what would have happened if he had arrested him, Simone said, "I reflected on this many times. And actually, if I had arrested him, I would have cuffed him, put him in the car, towed his motorcycle away and took him to jail. But there'd have been no reason to go to his house."

*   *   *

I still can't grasp it. I can't begin to count the times this sick fuck clanked Coronas with me, shared some of his weed, and even thanked me for watching his house. Yes, he thanked me for watching his damn house. Didn't make a whole lot of sense back then, and I don't know what I did that he appreciated, but I guess it all makes some shitty sense now.

Let's face it. Ariel was a sick fuck. When I use the term "sick" as in "sick fuck" I'm not implying that the bastard was actually sick. When standing his shaky ass before the judge at his sentencing hearing, Ariel claimed he was sick. No, he was a sick fuck. There's a huge difference. If someone's sick, they need to go to a mental hospital, get loaded up on Thorazine, and get cured. If someone's a sick fuck, they need to go to a prison where I spent time, and trust me, within the first few hours me and my homies would have cured that sick fuck with our own version of prison justice.

Actually, I wish Ariel would have never gone to prison. Let me explain. If there were real justice in America, here's what would have happened.

Amanda bangs on the door. I kick it in, and Amanda says there's two other girls in there. I yell in there, "Girls, get the hell out of here." They come out on the front porch, and I say, "OK, you ladies are free. Go on home." Then I would go down the street and gather up a few friends. We go back to Ariel's house, put everything back together like it was, and wait for him. He comes home, comes down in the basement, and we jump him. We bash the fuck out of him, chain him up, then each take our turn impregnating him. Then we starve him and kick the hell out of him and jump on his stomach until he aborts our babies through his hairy ass. Then we repeat the process for 10 years or so until we get tired of it and just forget about him. Or, more simply, as I said on "The Rock Newman Show," I would have separated his head from his body and kicked it down Seymour Avenue like a soccer ball. Either way would have been justice, and there would have been no need to bother the police or further clog up the judicial system.

*   *   *

On August 1, Ariel made his last public appearance as he attended his four-hour sentencing hearing. I later saw video of the most captivating moment, when Michelle, who had been held the longest and endured the worst of what this monster dished out, stood before him and delivered a most courageous speech.

"I remember all the times," she said softly, "you came home talking about what everybody else did wrong and acted like you wasn't doing the same thing. You said, 'At least I didn't kill you.' You took 11 years of my life away, and I have got it back. I spent 11 years in hell. Now your hell is just beginning. I will overcome all that happened, but you will face hell for eternity. From this moment on, I will not let you define me or affect who I am. I will live on. You will die a little every day as you think about the 11 years and the atrocities you inflicted on us.

"What does God think of you hypocritically going to church every Sunday, coming home to torture us? The death penalty would be so much easier; you don't deserve that. You deserve to spend life in prison. I can forgive you but I'll never forget. With the guidance of God, I will prevail and help others who have suffered at the hands of another. I know there's a lot of people going through hard times, but we need to reach out a hand and hold them, and let them know they're being heard. After 11 years, I am finally being heard and it's liberating."

Ariel had one last chance to do the one last decent thing left. That would have been to sit there silently and come to grips with reality. Instead, the muthafucka took the opportunity to show that he ranks with the great sick fucks of all time. First, he blamed his ex-wife for causing the violence between them, saying he "couldn't get her to quiet down . . . She put her hands on me, and that's how I reacted, by putting my hands on her."

As far as all the rapes and beatings he dished out on the girls, that asshole went on to say, "Most of the sex that went on in the house, and probably all of it, was consensual. These allegations about being forced upon them, that is totally wrong. There was times they would ask me for sex. I did not prey on these women, I just acted on my sexual instincts because of my sexual addiction . . . As God is my witness, I never beat these women. I never tortured them." Michelle was right. The death penalty would have been too easy for that dickhead.

On September 3, I was fuckin' around on the East Side of town when my phone began to go wild. "Did you hear about Ariel?" my friends were asking me. Ariel had committed suicide by hanging himself with a bed sheet in his prison cell. The scummy bastard knew what was coming his way had he ever set foot in general population, and he was too chickenshit to face it. After a few calls, including a request to meet some TV reporters on Seymour to give my response, my phone went dead. I met with reporters on Seymour and gave a brief statement. That evening I went home and charged my phone. When I checked my voicemail, there were a dozen or so desperate calls from Gino.

"Don't give any interviews!" he said. "I have one of the networks in New York willing to pay you $10,000 for your statement if it's an exclusive. Don't say anything to anyone else!"

Ah, fuck.

Ariel managed to turn this nightmare into a really bad Dracula movie. When you watch a Dracula movie, you know Dracula is going to get it in the brutal and bloody final scene. But by ending has last scene with a dirty bed sheet around his neck, that bastard Ariel was able to pull off the crime of the century without really feeling the force of justice. A more fitting ending to this story would be to have his greasy ass fried on an electric chair. Better yet, make him take a long shower, give him no towel, then fry him up. Or, had it been my decision as to what to do with him, I would have told him the case was dismissed, put him up in a luxury hotel, hired two strippers and put them in the pool. I'm sure Ariel would have found them quickly. As soon as he would have entered the pool, I'd have the strippers jump out, then I'd throw in a microwave oven and enjoy the fireworks show. Have a *muy caliente* time, asshole.

STOP THE MADNESS

Approximately 1 in 4 women in the United States (24.3%) has experienced severe physical violence by an intimate partner in her lifetime.
— 2010 National Intimate Partner and Sexual Violence Survey Centers for Disease Control and Prevention and the National Center for Injury Prevention and Control

THE EVENTS OF THE past year have changed my life for the better, and I am considerably blessed. I feel it's important that I find ways to make life better for others in whatever way I can.

My history of domestic violence is no secret. It is an ugly and odious part of my past. We all have things in our past that are regrettable, and for me, the terrible things I did to my wife hang over me every day. It is something I will probably never be able to shake off, a burden I never will be able to get out from under. Nor should it be. Perhaps someone will learn from one of the darkest parts of my life to look for the signs of abuse before it happens, and to have the courage to not be a victim anymore if it already has. Take this segment as part instructional, part confessional.

Abusers don't wear a scarlet A anywhere, and they can come in the most handsome packages. They don't have to be street thugs or addicts. They can be doctors, lawyers, cooks, teachers, preachers—anyone. One of the first things abusers do is look for the easy target. Abusers want someone who is weak, vulnerable, and with low self-esteem. A strong, confident woman will ward off many abusers at the start. They need a handy and convenient victim.

Beware of the guy who suddenly swamps you with affection and gifts. It's a way to see how strong or weak you are. It also is a way to create the illusion that you are indebted to him. The abuser wants you to let your guard down and think that he's going to take care of your every need. And when you start thinking that, he'll start demanding that he takes care of every detail of your life. Pretty soon he'll control every aspect of your life—where you go, who you can talk to, what you watch on television. He'll demand to know who you're talking to on the phone, who you're texting, and who you're emailing. Bit by bit you lose control of your life. It doesn't happen overnight. It's a step-by-step process, and it will consume you before you realize it happened.

We humans tend to be mimicking creatures. We repeat what we see. What we see in the home when we are young becomes the standard of "normal." So instead of being awestruck by a new man's smothering affection, here's a good question to ask: "Tell me how your father treated your mother." Then just stay silent. The answer he gives will be most telling. You can take it to the bank that the way his father treated his mother is exactly what's in store for you. Even if he says, "Dad was bad to Mom, but I would never be that way," don't believe it. He may actually not want to repeat the terrible things he saw his father do to his mother, but when difficult times come, and they will in every relationship, he will quickly revert back to what he perceives as "normal." You must do everything possible to prevent yourself from accepting that as "normal."

Beware of any guy who rants on and on about how bad his exes are. Don't buy it if he says he was a victim of abuse by women, or if he claims women falsely accused him of abuse. He quickly becomes very sexually demanding, and sexually very selfish.

"If I get with him, he'll change." This is a familiar song, and you couldn't be more wrong. This has got to be one of the most common and costly mistakes women make. Men are creatures of habit, and our traits, good and bad, are hard-wired into our heads. Here again, a man might say, "Yes, baby, I'll change for you," and he might actually want to, but 99 percent of the time he won't.

Something positive to look for: If his parents are still together, and yours are, too, the standard has been set very high and the chance the relationship will work out is pretty good. But if you both come from broken homes, the chance of you both repeating the pattern is very high.

One of the sure signs that abuse is coming is jealous, controlling behavior. You might first think it's a sign of love, but it isn't. It's a sign that he considers you his possession, not an individual. You begin to believe his very short fuse and explosive temper are the result of something you did wrong. And of course, nothing is his fault. Everything that goes wrong is because you're stupid. Then he slams doors, punches walls, or throws furniture or objects around. Believe me, baby, you're next.

When the relationship first began, your heart fluttered as you told everyone what a wonderful, caring, doting man you found. Now you are too embarrassed to admit that you were fooled, and that now you're trapped. Your friends and family see it. They plead with you to do something. But you dismiss their concerns. Your situation is different. "Why do you stay with him?" they ask. "Because I love him," you timidly reply. Baby, you have no idea what love is. You don't love him. You're dependent on him. No different than how a crackhead feels about cocaine.

Don't take it. Don't put up with it. Even when he says, "Oh, baby, I'm sorry, I'm sorry, I'm sorry," don't fall for it. When it comes to domestic violence, make it one and you're done. Sometimes giving a guy a second or third chance is OK if it's because he's made a mistake or did something stupid. Forgiveness, reconciliation and restoration are all morally superior whenever possible. But if he hits you once, just once, unless you get out of the relationship then and there, he will come at you again and again. When it comes to domestic violence, it's one and done. No second chances. None.

It's not your fault. There's nothing you can do to change it, and for God's sake you aren't going to change him. Take the kids and get out, *now*. There's plenty of places to go, plenty of people and organizations that will help you. It takes courage that you don't think you have, and strength you think you lost long ago, but reach down for that last shred of self-respect and get yourself out of that situation. And then don't let him back in. Ever. Don't listen when he begs and pleads and swears that he's changed. Millions have fallen for that, and way too many are now in graves.

If I've just described your situation, you know you should take action, but you're scared. You're trapped in a hell that you're too scared to try to escape. Don't fall for thinking "I'll never do better than him." That's a crock. And yes, your kids need a father, but a real father, not just a sperm donor. If you stay with this bastard you're just breeding the next generation of abusers. Let this be the day this toothless dishwasher kicked down your front door. But remember, while I may have kicked down the door, the girls still walked out on their own. You need to find the strength to do that as well.

I am taking up the cause of helping women get out of abusive relationships. I will be lending whatever celebrity status I may have to aid women's shelters around the country. It is my hope that we can build and/or support shelters in every state. This is my small way of righting a terrible wrong in my life.

WHO'S STEREOTYPING NOW?

> Of course the problem [of racism] is not solved . . . I said this,
> you know, for apartheid, South Africa, I said this for my own com-
> munity in the South—there are still generations of people, older
> people, who were born and bred and marinated in it, in that prej-
> udice and racism, and they just have to die.
> —Oprah Winfrey

ONE OF THE MAIN reasons my part in this whole event became
such an international story is the series of ironies that didn't fit the
usual stereotypical patterns and perceptions. This time the scary
black dude turned out to be the good guy. And this same scary
black dude turned out to be more of a funny guy on TV rather
than a thuggish street rat. Plus this scary lookin' black dude spoke
openly about the race factor.

In a perfect world it shouldn't matter what race I was or what
race the girls were. But we don't live in a perfect world. Race still
plays a factor in society's perception of what should and shouldn't
be. Deep inside, everyone knows that. I was just the first one in a
long time to actually say it to the world, and with a goofy smile.

Let's adjust the location and add some bleach. If I were a white
dude with perfect teeth walking down Wolf Road in the upscale
Cleveland suburb of Bay Village and found the girls in someone's
four-bedroom colonial, yes, it would have made the news, but
not to this extent. Yes, I would have gotten a certificate of appre-
ciation from the mayor or something nice like that, but would I
have become more popular in the Philippines than King Rajah
Matanda? Would Anderson Cooper have flown out to interview

me? Would Snoop Dogg have called me and invited me to be on his show? Would McDonald's have given me so much as an upgrade to a large order of fries? (By the way, contrary to popular belief, I do not have lifetime free hamburgers at McDonald's. They did give me $1,000 in gift cards, which I just passed out to kids in the neighborhood.)

Throughout this book I have used the term "nigga" many times. If that bothers you, well, hell, your breathing bothers me. First of all, in the black world, the term "nigga" can be construed as a term of endearment. If a one white dude calls another white dude "pal," it could be good or it could be bad. "Hey, pal, thanks for the lift to the country club," is a nice way white people use the word "pal." But if a white dude says, "Hey, pal, you're wearing the wrong dinner jacket," well, that's a slur. Black folks on the streets who are friends call each other nigga all the time. Besides, in this book, who have I referred to as "nigga" almost every time? Donny Osmond? No, it's been me. When Snoop Dogg and I called each other "nigga" when he called to congratulate me, hell, it was an honor. So you holier-than-thou whiny critics: just shut it. Go find something worthwhile to get all uppity about.

Now, if you really want to offend me, don't call me "nigga," call me "African-American." That's a stupid, loathsome term, because being an American means we are all *Americans*. Not hyphenated Americans. Just plain Americans. "Americans" is the term that unites us. When you start putting all these stupid qualifiers in front of it, that's what divides us.

Let me tell you all a thing or two about racism. In my world, until this rescue, when I would walk into a convenience store, people would grab their children and duck out the door. For me, it's a good day if I can get past the West 25th Street crackheads and make it to McDonald's. My reality has been boarding houses and prison cells.

Many in the media are much better-looking and much smoother talkers than I will ever be, yet they have no clue what racism is. I've seen it and lived in it every day, and it doesn't come from some old Southern geezer who didn't want to drink out of the same water fountain as us coloreds 60 years ago. It has taken on a kinder, gentler, yet most insidious form cloaked as compassion. Our oppressors have swapped the shackles and chains of slavery for shackles and chains of government dependency. We are no longer exploited in the cotton fields of Georgia; instead we are exploited in the halls of government.

The great civil rights victories of the 1950s and 1960s were resisted every step of the way by whom? Those mean racist Republicans? Let's review our history. It was the Democrat Party that defended slavery. It was the Democrat Party that brought us Jim Crow, Dred Scott and Plessy v. Ferguson. (Yes, I call it the Democrat Party instead of the Democratic Party because there's very little that's democratic about it. I'm just being philosophically and grammatically more honest.) It was the Democrat Party that brought us the Ku Klux Klan. It was the Democrat Party that put a former Klansman on the Supreme Court (Hugo Black) and in the White House (Harry Truman). It was the Democrat Party that gave us segregation today, segregation tomorrow, segregation forever. It was the Democrat Party that brought us the poll tax, literacy tests, and as recently as 1987 installed a former Klansman as majority leader of the United States Senate (Robert Byrd). It's the Democrat Party that forced this debacle of Obamacare down our throats and demanded the Internal Revenue Service investigate those who object.

And when justice overcame the ignorance and hate, their strategy shifted. Our brothas and sistas were no longer being controlled with snarling dogs, fire hoses, and Bull Connor. Instead, we were rounded up into virtual internment camps, disguised as a war on poverty. In reality it was a war on our independence. The government then gave us just enough food and just enough goodies to keep us alive. If that were a temporary measure to help people who were down and out, that would be a good thing. But the purpose behind it was to buy black America's votes and then keep us dependent. It worked. It was Lyndon Johnson who said, "I'll have those niggers voting Democratic for the next 200 years," after signing the "war on poverty" legislation. Not this nigga. I've seen the destruction and havoc it has rained on our people. I wouldn't vote for a Democrat if my life depended on it. Racism is imbued within liberalism. If you buy one, you bought the other, whether you meant to or not.

Our people have been taught to get everything they can out of the government instead of taking advantage of the great opportunities this country offers. Our brothas and sistas have been turned into government-dependent junkies. Why should someone go get an education and a job when the government will pay for their housing through Section 8, pay for their food through food stamps, pay for their healthcare through Medicaid, and provide them with crack money through welfare and supplemental security income? Need more money? Make more babies!

We were suckered to vote for Barack Obama. Since he's been in office, things have only gotten worse for our people. This is the hope and change Barack Obama promised? Can you imagine the yelling and screaming had these things happened to us under George Bush or Ronald Reagan? Somewhere some Klansmen are snickering under their sheets with delight over what has happened to our people.

Yes, if you haven't figured it out yet, I'm a Republican. A proud and true Tea Partier. I'm not the kind you'll find at the wine-tasting society or the country club board of directors. I'm not well-groomed, I speak like a street thug, look like a street thug, got plenty of warts and did plenty of stupid un-Republican-like shit. I'm no war hero. I got my ass thrown out of the military on purpose instead of fighting. So I don't expect to be getting any invitations to speak at the next Republican Convention confab. But I don't buy into this pile of Barbra Streisand that the Democrat Party represents the best interest of black America. History, current events, and my street-level observations show just the opposite. I am the Democrats' worst nightmare: a black man who thinks for himself.

*   *   *

After the rescue, when everyone on the Internet was going crazy, some T-shirt company in St. Louis started selling a "Charles Ramsey for President" shirt. Now if I were elected president, ah, yes, things would get done. For Vice President, I'd choose among three brilliant Caucasian dudes: Anderson Cooper, John Walsh, or Brian Williams. Any of them would be good. The first staff person I'd appoint would be Howard Stern as my press secretary. I can't think of anyone who would be more effective to stand in front of the press corps and tell them they're a bunch of dickwads and then just walk away.

Here are some cabinet secretary appointments I would make:

Secretary of Defense. This one is easy. I'd pick Dave Chappelle. Dave is unpredictable, a bit nutty, a bit over the top, and that's the kind of crazy bastard we need sitting next to the red button. I'd keep him sleep- and cigarette-deprived and amped up on Red Bull, with a Chappelle cam constantly trained on him so that lil' fuck Kim Jong Un would think twice about doin' any stupid shit.

Secretary of Commerce. I'd put Warren Buffett here. He found a way to make billions of dollars; I'm sure he could teach the rest of American business how to as well.

Secretary of Energy. Rush Limbaugh is one of the smartest bastards in America and would fit well into any cabinet post. But what a delight it would be to see that already blubbery cotton-ass Al Gore turn whiter than a polar bear's ass in an arctic snowstorm if Rush were in charge of America's energy development.

Attorney General. This is another no-brainer. It would be my boy Snoop Dogg. He'd bring peace between the Bloods and the Crips and make America one hell of a happy party town.

Secretary of State. I was thinking about Dennis Rodman, but that's been tried already. Any black dude who could pull off playing me on his show has what it takes to broker international peace deals. This is a job for Mike Epps.

Secretary of Treasury. Puff Daddy. The man thinks twenty-dollar bills are just a form of litter. That's the kind of thinking we need there.

Secretary of Agriculture. This is a rather boring position, so to liven things up, I'll put in Jim Carrey, in full Fire Marshal Bill character.

Ambassador to the United Nations. Drew Carey. Drew once told me to love everyone, so I figure he'd be able to tell the rest of the world the same.

And what would be some of the things I'd do as president? For starters, I'd triple the defense budget, at least, so that the rest of the world knows not to fuck with us. I wouldn't put our soldiers in harm's way unless there is a distinct and clear American interest at stake. I don't care if one Arab is blowing up another Arab—they've been doing that for centuries and they'll continue to do so for the next dozen centuries. I'd develop our own energy reserves and tell all those Mideast tyrants to just go to hell. I'd keep guns but ban criminals. As for the gay marriage debate: I don't give a shit if two dudes or two chicks want to play crouching tiger hidden dragon. Just call it something else other than marriage.

I'll make some quick, overdue decisions that will clean up a lot of the shit that's been coming out of Washington. Yes, I can see the day: The chief justice of the Supreme Court swears me in, the cannons go off, and I approach the podium to deliver the greatest inaugural address ever.

Quoting those sweet words my mother said to me for all those years, I would say so reverently, "My fellow Americans, JUST WHAT THE FUCK'S THE MATTER WITH YOU?

"America, have you lost your ever-lovin' fuckin' mind? Just what the hell did you expect when you put my predecessor in office? Peace? Prosperity? Hope? A Browns Super Bowl? Look at the shithole this country has turned into, and look at how we got here. You were all pissin' your pants in excitement of Barack Obumma becoming president: now look where we are. America, JUST WHAT THE FUCK'S THE MATTER WITH YOU?

"It didn't take more than a few years for this guy to rack up more debt than all previous presidents combined. Never since the Great Depression has unemployment been this high this fuckin' long. The United States has fallen from a completely free nation to a 'mostly free nation.' America, JUST WHAT THE FUCK'S THE MATTER WITH YOU?

"We've got all this damn oil under our feet. We've got all this damn coal under our feet. We've got enough energy to tell the Arabs to all go to hell and we'd never have to send another kid to get his balls shot off in the Middle East. Yet, we can't develop our own independent resources. We've been wasting zillions of dollars on crony bankrupt green energy shit. America, JUST WHAT THE FUCK'S THE MATTER WITH YOU?

"We freed the slaves 150 years ago. But we re-enslaved them with all these government handouts that created a damn permanent dependent underclass. Anybody who questions the poor decisions of a black man is called a racist. And black men and women who dare to tell the truth are shunned or destroyed. America, JUST WHAT THE FUCK'S THE MATTER WITH YOU?

"This nation has had the greatest and most accessible health-care system in the world. Homeless people can get treatment at the same hospitals and from the same doctors as visiting rag-headed Saudi royalty. The last thing we wanted was for the government to ram down our throats a hideously expensive system we didn't need and that is canceling more insurance policies than it's issuing to the uninsured. But that's what the fuck we got with Obamacare. We were told to pass the fuckin' bill so we could find out what the fuck was in it. We did, and boy did we fuckin' ever. America, WHAT THE FUCK'S THE MATTER WITH YOU?

"Illegal aliens flood across our borders, enticed by all the goddamn free giveaways waiting for them and the willingness of goddamn politicians to look the other way. We know why they do this—those fuckin' spineless politicians see these poor souls as future members of the Democrat Party. America, WHAT THE FUCK'S THE MATTER WITH YOU?

"But not to worry, dear Americans. I have simple solutions that I plan to implement much in the same manner my predecessor implemented his ideas when he couldn't get his crazyshit ideas past Congress. A few strokes of my pen upon a few executive orders and America will once again be all the hot shit it used to be. The first thing I will do is ban racism. That's right. I'll ban racism. Now who of you all would be opposed to that? And the fastest and most efficient way to ban racism is to ban the Democrat Party. Yep, that's the party that brought us slavery, Jim Crow, segregation, and all that bullshit that held us black people back. Now they expect us all to be slavish in loyalty to them by making us dependent on the government. No fuckin' way, America. To get rid of racism, we need to get rid of the party that brought it to us.

"The second thing I'll do is ban poverty. Again, who of you out there is for poverty? Not me. There again, the fastest way to ban poverty is to ban the Democrat Party. With all the insanely high taxes we all have to pay, and considering the fact that American business pays the highest business taxes in the free world, it's no wonder this county is shittin' out jobs to Mexico and elsewhere. And when otherwise healthy people believe this country owes them a living instead of taking advantage of the opportunities that abound, well that breeds poverty. We need to stop throwing money at it and start demanding accountability of those who perpetuate this shit on us.

"The next thing I'll do is ban war. Again, the best way to do that is to ban the Democrat Party. That's the party that got us into the War of 1812, the Civil War, the Mexican War, World War I, World War II, Korea, and Vietnam. I'll triple the size of our military so that no tin-horned pissant dictator would ever dream of fucking with us. But the Democrats want to piss our money away on such gems like near-useless windmills, examining and measuring the reproductive organs of male ducks, studying why three-quarters of lesbians in the United States are overweight and why most gay males are not, teaching Moroccans how to design and make pottery, and purchasing talking urinal cakes up in Michigan. Yep, those are real things our fuckin' politicians spent your fuckin' money on.

"I promise to cut taxes. Not this supply-side nonsense we tried before, when after we cut tax rates we saw tax revenues soar. What a fuckin' rip-off. These assholes in Washington just spent it on other stupid shit. If we cut taxes and the damn government still gets more fuckin' money, we didn't cut them the fuck enough.

"You all don't think I can do all this shit? You think there's some sort of restriction in the Constitution? Well, if there is or isn't, I sure don't give a fuck, because the clown I'm replacing sure didn't either. If you disagree with me, well, obviously, since I'm black, you must be a racist! Question me and I'll have the Internal Revenue Service audit your ugly racist ass.

"Now for my black brothas and sistas, GOOD NEWS! I support

reparations to ya all. Yes! Millions, billions! After the Democrat Party is permanently banned, I shall use my powers as president to seize all their assets and sell them off and distribute the cash to ya all. I'm sure they've got nice cribs around the country, and once we sell them all off, there's going to be one hell of a party, because we'll be free from our oppressors at last!

Thank you, and God bless America!"

CARDS AND LETTERS

There must be millions of people all over the world who never get any love letters . . . I could be their leader.
—Charlie Brown

THE CARDS AND LETTERS from around the world came flooding in by the thousands. Some were quick thank-you cards, others tried to tell me their life's story. Poems. Stories. Small donations, large donations, hundreds of gift cards. Some requested autographs, some people wanted me to respond in essay form. A note on the envelope of a letter from New York warned the mailman, "You better get this right!"

I also got a shirt and a nice note from Jennifer Lee Pryor, widow of the great comedian Richard Pryor. "I'm sure my husband would have appreciated you and your honesty as I do," she wrote.

With all the hoopla that followed in the months after the rescue, I didn't get the chance to sit down and read them all until recently. My God, I am overwhelmed. This hardened street thug broke into tears reading all those cards and letters, especially the hundreds that came from children. I literally received hundreds of letters from children of all ages, and many of them included some very creative artwork. There's a picture of me standing among angels; there are several pictures of me breaking down the door. A picture showing me standing in a flower field with the girls. Another picture showed me in a Superman getup with CR on my chest and a McDonald's bag in my hand. Another had me dressed as Batman with "CR" shining in the sky like the bat signal.

One person told me that I was now in his will. A couple of prisoners wrote me, saying I was a hero among those incarcerated. Some women wanted to know if I was married. A guy in Florida wanted to buy the shirt I wore during the rescue.

I cannot express the gratitude I feel for each and every one of these cards and letters. I will hang on to these forever. They mean more to me than any possession on earth. I just wish I could personally thank everyone who shared their love with me. You have humbled me deeply, and as you can tell from the adventures in this book, that is a very hard thing to do.

Here is a very small sample of the notes and letters that flooded me with your love.

Charles: You are cool, funny, and awesome. I'd like to hang out with you. Your friend, Noah

I just wanna say I love your sense of humor. All your interviews made me laugh. You are so funny and cool. But yeah, I'm glad you helped. Much Respect to you!
Love, Candace Graham, Lumberton, NC

Mr. Charles—I've seen your interview videos and I must say what you did was a very good thing. I'm sure those three girls and their families are thankful that you helped them. In my opinion, I think you are a kindhearted guy and I have much respect for you. Sincerely, Katrina, North Carolina

Samuel L. Jackson is the coolest, but he ain't got nothing on Charles Ramsey! —Hugh Slusser, Virginia Beach, VA

With all the less than pleasant news in the world you helped immensely at putting a happy smile on peoples' faces worldwide. God bless you! Thank you!
—The Parsons Family, Phoenix, AZ

I saw you on TV and you have touched so many people with your humility and kindness. You stepped up to the plate and God used you in an extraordinary way! God bless you. —Bev Kish

Thank you so much for being a good man and a great neighbor! We in California are grateful for you. —Toni N.

You sir are a hero, and I am just so happy for you!
—Edwin, New Jersey

You are a wonderful and humble man. You are REAL and we are so impressed with your down to earth attitude. God bless you!
—Angelina

I heard you being interviewed by the media and let me say this, keep on being you, Charles!
—Three Proud Americans from Chicago

Charles, we love you here in San Francisco, CA! You are brave.
—(unsigned)

Thank you Mr. Ramsey—you are a fine human being, THE REAL DEAL! I send you my gratitude and love and I pray that any troubles you have will lessen soon. —Wendy

Thank you for putting up with America's outpouring of love! Because, Dude, you have added a dimension to Mother's Day 2013 that was unimaginable until that day. Thank you from every mom in America! Soak up the love! From: All the women I know. —(unsigned)

What you did was wonderful. In today's world no one wants to get involved. We will never forget. May God bless you!
—Jim and Faith Stevens, Dunbar, WV

I really enjoyed your interview with Anderson Cooper. You are very real and smart! Thanks for what you did and stay real. —
Danny Popkin, Pennington, NJ

Within 24 hours of the rescue, the cards and letter poured in from all over the world, probably giving the mailman a hernia. *(Randy Nyerges)*

Thank you for being such a stand-up guy. May God bless you.
—The Delong Family, Long Beach, CA

Thank you for doing the right thing. I know that you don't like to hear this, but you are a hero. —Mary Hayes

Thank you for being one of the few brave men who actually care about your brothers and sisters, no matter what color.
—Larry and Kathy Smith

I feel safer knowing there are people like you in the world.
—Laura, Washington, DC

God put people on this earth for a reason, and you are an angel for those girls. Your honesty, courage, and humanness has touched my heart and the country's.
—Patty Hannel, Lancaster, NY

Your self sacrifice is an inspiration to us all and a reminder that we are our brothers keeper. May you be a role model to others.
—Rev. Luke Amadeo, Guadeloupe, West Indies

Bro, you are a HERO! I hope one million good Americans send you $5 each. Here is number one. 4,999,999 to go. Your bro in heart in Seattle. —Paul West, Auburn, WA

From here on out, nothing but good things are going to happen to you because you placed your life on the line in helping those girls. I can't stress enough how the people in the world are wishing you well, especially me!
—Mercedes Foster, Las Vegas, NV

Thank you for being such a strong and wonderful person. May God bless you for the rest of your life.
—Amy Day, Bryan, TX

I honestly believe you should be Time Magazine's Person of the Year 2013. —Ariel Rivera, Alburtis, PA

I received many wonderful letters from Mrs. Engle's second grade class at Berclair Elementary School in Memphis, Tennessee:

Charles Ramsey, you're a HERO. A true hero, just like Superman. I just want you to know I'm your biggest fan. —Victor McCoy

Cool. You save people. —Angel

Charles Ramsey, you are a hero! Thank u for saving Michelle Knight and Amanda Berry and Gina DeJesus. —Kadaiza

You're my hero for saving the girls. —Jocelyn Galarza

Thank you for saving them. —Shawdale Pixson

LET THE LOVE LIVE ON

I'M OFTEN ASKED, "HOW has this whole experience changed your life?" You may be surprised, but the answer is "very little." Yes, I get recognized and loved on by strangers almost every time I step outside, but I'm still me. I didn't gain any knowledge or acquire any superpowers or change what I like or who I like to hang around with. That's all the same. This whole story has impacted people around me more than it's affected me.

Stardom is something you work your ass off for. The rock star becomes a rock star by playing that guitar in his mother's basement hours on end. The professional athlete becomes a professional athlete by working his body hard, pushing it to the limit, making sacrifices along the way. A top chef becomes a top chef by reading every cookbook, watching every cooking show, experimenting with every recipe. They all worked years at what they do. I didn't. This whole thing fell out of the sky and landed on me. Why me? No one will ever know. As has been characteristic of my life, I walk into the drama. It doesn't walk to me.

Of course, people came out of the woodwork promising to guide me to riches and fame. With the exception of a very few, they were just looking to hitch themselves up to this roller coaster and go for the ride. There were plenty of people who were long on promises but very short on delivery. But there's not a whole lot I could do about that. I was a goddamn dishwasher, not a well-coached United States Senate candidate. I had no idea what advice was good or bad. I had not a fuckin' clue as to what was good media strategy. I had no idea what would be involved in writing a book. I had not a clue that my words would be analyzed by commentators and reporters around the world. I had no experience to draw from, no old friends who had been through something similar who could give me advice.

The girls got all sorts of free legal advice from one of the finest law firms in the country. They were protected by family, friends, lawyers, and policemen. And they should have been—good for them. I'm glad they got every good thing that came their way. The City of Cleveland was having its greatest moment of civic pride since the Browns won the world title in 1964. Everyone was finding a way to cash in on this amazing event—except me. When the happy train left the station, I was left on the platform.

I don't have free hamburgers for life. I don't have free french fries for life. Those were never offered to me, but most folk seem to think so. There were plenty of opportunistic bastards who tried to use my likeness to cash in. There was a Charles Ramsey action figure, scores of T-shirts, even a video game. These were all done without my consent, and I never made a dime from them. I did get a lawyer who helped me trademark my likeness and put an end to those who were trying to capitalize on it, and collected a whole $500 in damages. Now I don't mind people trying to find a way to make a buck, but if they're using my likeness I certainly need to be a part of it.

I did get a kick out of the guy who tattooed my face on his leg. Since he wasn't making any money on it, I took it as a compliment.

After the first media barrage had passed, it was time for life to try to get back to normal. But that was next to impossible. I was fortunate that I had several options as to where to live, and I had a few dollars in the bank. It wasn't like I could just return to a desk job in the accounting department. Everywhere I went I caused a disruption, which kept potential employers from hiring me even for the most menial jobs. Technically, I am homeless, but only because I don't own a home. I have plenty of places that I call home, and I move among them as needed. I plan to live this way from this point on, no matter if I become a millionaire or return to dishwashing.

I was invited to a New Year's Eve VIP reception in Cleveland, which was attended by Drew Carey. When I was introduced to Drew, his face lit up as he gave me a big handshake and bear hug. "Wow, it's great to meet someone who's made Cleveland more famous than I did," Drew said. We had a great conversation, with Drew doing most of the talking, but he was giving me great advice on handling my celebrity status.

"Now everyone is your neighbor," he said. "Everyone loves you, everyone wants to be a part of you. So just love them back as best you can."

In February 2014 I met up with Snoop Dogg for a weekend when he performed in Cincinnati. Snoop invited me up to his suite before the show. We embraced like long-lost brothers, and Snoop said he hopes that my adventure would help rescue other women out there. Along with Snoop was Daz Dillinger, and we all had a good time on Snoop's bus.

As for what's next for me, it's hard to say. I was contacted to do a series of stand-up comedy routines. That's something I've enjoyed doing since the first grade, except back then those routines would get me suspended from school. Will these actually happen? Who knows? I've been contacted about a reality TV show, and as of this writing a pilot is in the works. Will there be a movie deal? Again, who knows? But I certainly could see myself accepting an Academy Award someday. I have trusted, professional people in place who are working on developing my newfound entertainment career.

This grand adventure has opened doors for me, but success isn't automatic. My notoriety might get me in the door, but I will have to prove that I actually belong on the A list.

I'm still numbed by this experience, as if I slammed down a five-gallon jug of Novocain. I still can't grasp why people stop me on the street to get a picture, and why a small-scale riot erupts when I walk in public, like through Tower City Center downtown. Hardened criminals come up to me and give me hug, saying stuff like, "What you did is so beautiful" while choking on their words.

I was driving downtown and got into a minor car wreck. The woman in the other car jumped out, screaming and swearing at me like some sort of psychobitch. But when I got out, she noticed it was me, and just like that she went from screamin' bitch to adoring fan. I didn't get a ticket for the accident, but I did get a big hug.

A few months after the rescue I saved another white woman, this time from her own stupidity. I was getting gas at a Marathon station of the east side of Cleveland, when I noticed a woman sitting in her car yappin' on her cell phone. The problem was that she hadn't noticed that something went wrong with the auto shut-off and gas was splashing down the side of her damn car. I saw it, so I waved and yelled at the dude in the booth, who just stared at me, probably thinking I was just flippin' out on angel dust. So I ran toward the woman's car, stopping about 10 feet short. I didn't want her to think some crazed black dude was trying to attack her, and besides, the gas was beginning to pool on the ground. I yelled at the woman, who glanced at me while still chattering away on her phone.

"There's gas all over the place!" I yelled at her. "Your fuckin' car is leaking gas everywhere!"

She looked down through the window and let out a shriek. The gas was pumping full blast and spewing out the tank like Niagara Falls. The woman opened the door and stepped out, soaking her UGGs almost to the ankles. She just stood there, blank stare on her face, not knowing what to do. I then ran over to the hose and clicked off the latch.

Chillin' with my boy Snoop Dogg in his hotel suite before a concert in Cincinnati.
(Jennifer Baker)

"Oh, dear God," she said. "Thank you."
"No problem," I said. "You look a bit shaky. Need a cigarette?"

*　　　*　　　*

We hear the story of the horror these girls endured and ask the rhetorical question: "Why do bad things happen to good people?" To that I now add, "Why do good things happen to bad people?"

That's a mystery we'll never solve.

After all the crazy shit that was my life before the rescue and the other crazy shit that followed, you might think I'm a different person. But no, I'm not. I'm not any smarter; maybe just a bit wiser. Nothing in this whole experience has restored any faith in humanity; in fact I still can't believe the incredible stupidity I still see all around me. Just flip on the television and you'll see what I mean.

Nothing in this world has really changed. Children are still being gunned down while playing on inner-city streets. Other children are still being snatched away and terrorized. Women are still being abused. Screwballs are blowing up people in the name of God. For a few days in May 2013, we forgot about all that shit. It seemed like it came to a halt. But it didn't.

It's an old saying, but it's true: The only thing that is constant is change. Look back at your life. Five years ago, would you have predicted your life is what it is now? I doubt it. Whether your life is better or worse, you can't change the past, but you can change the future. Every time I got myself into deep shit, I found a way out. I just may have taken a more jagged path than you.

You never know what surprises await you around the corner, or for that matter, in your neighbor's basement. You never know when you, with all your defects, will be called upon by whatever higher power to do something extraordinary. And you don't have to have any special talents or education to do something amazing. Look at me. I kicked in a door, and the world freaked out.

*   *   *

Thank you all, from my innermost being. Walk in love, dear brothas and sistas, and keep America safe.

ONE MORE THING: HAMBURGERS

I'VE ALWAYS LOVED HAMBURGERS. Other than a steak, burgers have been my favorite meat. My favorites are from McDonald's. (I was trying to chomp down a Big Mac when Amanda forever interrupted things.) I also like the burgers at Red Robin.

But grilled burgers are always great, too. And not some frozen meat disc you throw on the grill. Get a pound of ground Angus. While it might not be the leanest meat, it certainly is the tastiest. Then mix it in a bowl with about ¼ cup of Worcestershire Sauce and ¼ cup A-1 Sauce. But I usually don't go to the trouble of measuring it out—I just throw everything into a bowl and mix it up. Then roll the mixture into balls and then flatten them out into patties. Ah yes. Then carefully put them on the grill and cook them about seven minutes on each side, flipping only once. If you flip them more than once they could fall apart.

When done, put them on high-quality buns, not the cheapo shit. Good buns, with sesame seeds, and grilled with a little butter is even better. Some folks of course like lettuce, tomato, onion, etc. Whatever suits your taste, folks, pile it on. This is America.

ACKNOWLEDGMENTS

SPECIAL THANKS TO LIL Wayne, Mo'Nique, Al Sharpton, Stuart Scott, 2 Chainz, Snoop Dogg, Drew Carey, Anderson Cooper, John Walsh, Eric Conn, Rock Newman, the Pratt Family, the Gresham Family, Jenn Baker, Mike Trivisonno, the Walker & Jocke Law Firm, the Guardian Angels, the FBI, the Cleveland Police, the Gregory Brothers, Gray & Company Publishers, McDonald's, Mike Epps, L.C., the state of Oregon, the nations of Australia and Sweden.

And a big thanks to Jane-Ann Nyerges for being the glue that made this whole project stick together.

ABOUT THE CO-AUTHOR

RANDY NYERGES IS A freelance writer and a former staff member of the United States Senate. He is co-author of the books "Day of the Dawg," with Hanford Dixon, and "The Studio," with Hikia. He resides in Berea, Ohio.

> For news and updates, visit:
> **www.CharlesRamseyWorld.com**

For news and updates, visit:
www.CharlesRamseyWorld.com